THE ROYAL
HERITAGE
COOKBOOK

THE ROYAL HERITAGE COOKBOOK

RECIPES FROM HIGH SOCIETY AND THE ROYAL COURT

The Hon. Sarah Macpherson

The
History
Press

First published 2015

The History Press
The Mill, Brimscombe Port
Stroud, Gloucestershire, GL5 2QG
www.thehistorypress.co.uk

British Library Cataloguing in Publication Data.
A catalogue record for this book is available from the British Library.

ISBN 978 0 7509 6394 7

Typesetting and origination by The History Press
Printed and bound in Malta, by Melita Press.

Contents

Starters

Light Lunches

Main Courses

Family Meals

Curries

Desserts

Cakes

Notes

Acknowledgements

My personal thanks and acknowledgement to:

The wonderful members of our Historic Cooks Company: Carole Awnack, Wendy Bailey, Ros Blount, Chris Carr, Sarah Cozens, Sue Wynne Davies, Kate Hunloke, Maeve Hunt, Ginnie Keen, Jane Lees-Millais, Jeni McGregor, Jan Penn, Jan Pink, Jenny Potter (Dunford), Jophy Powell, Jennie Shaw, Ros Spicer, Jo and Annette Whitworth, Juliet Wilmot and Joyce Wood.

Deborah Loader, historic cook and personal assistant; Francis Pearson, wine merchant, for constant and wise advice; Paul Whitaker, chairman of the Pink Elephant Club of Bristol Dining Committee, and his predecessor, Mike Dowdeswell; Hilary Pearson and Lizzie and Colin Legge, historic cook leaders and advisers; Sandy Bagnall, historic cook leader; Emma Fourie (Maitland-Carew) for videos of the secrets of Thirlestane Castle, and Lisa Saunders, of All About Cupcakes, cake decorator.

Elizabeth Gibb, Meg Holbrook and Marlene Lewis, compilers for the Lacock Papers; Claire Skinner and Mike Marshman of Wiltshire and Swindon History Centre, for all their support with Lacock Abbey Papers; all the staff at Wiltshire and Swindon History Centre and the volunteers of the 'Lacock Unlock' project.

Cllr Richard Tonge, Wiltshire County Council; Professor Ron George, Lacock Parish Council; Katherine Manning and Ann Cox, Lacock Abbey National Trust Administration; Stephen Wundke of Swirrel Mas, adviser and food festival organiser; Sarah and Matthew Jackson, The Red Lion, Lacock; Jenny Rowlands, public lectures assistant; Anna Blundell-Williams, for her design advice; Ronan Colgan, Beth Amphlett, Chris West and the team at The History Press; Katherine and Markus Bolder, for all their technical and computer help; Caroline Gray, cookery adviser and party organiser; Ian Macpherson, my editor and cheese consultant, for his love and endless support and Nick Brink of Carlton Books Ltd at Carlton Publishing House, for arranging the rights to include extracts from *Court Favourites* by Elizabeth Craig (Andre Deutsch, 1953).

The professional recipe testing and advice from gourmet restaurateurs Neil and Sarah at the Foxham, Wiltshire, has been invaluable. They have my grateful thanks.

And a special acknowledgement to Andy Crump of K. & E.J. Crump & Son, Royal Wootton Bassett, for their generous meat sponsorship.

Introduction

As a domestic historian, I have published books on my own family history as well as recently discovered National Trust old recipes and remedies used by the upstairs and downstairs life inside a great house of bygone years.

The National Trust has yet again allowed me to open a Pandora's Box in Wiltshire - an entire chest of untouched manuscripts! Opening the lid of the box, I found a treasure trove of royal and noble recipes from approximately 300 years ago.

A unique history of cooking was revealed as I reached inside to find written proof of King Charles ll's favourite food (sirloin, and apple and apricot pie) and King James ll's favourite teacake, along with another 1,500 forgotten recipes.

I determined to convert the best of these into an up-to-date 'book of royal recipes'; some were suitable to be used almost straight from the manuscript, for family lunches, others needed a bit of work to bring them up to date, while others still have provided the inspiration for new dinner party dishes. I have also made extensive use of their knowledge of alcohol, marinating, and herbs in creating these wonderful dishes.

Many of the recipes in the box were almost unreadable, many were faded, and many were written at a time before properly standardised written English, so much of the spelling was quite incredible.

They revealed an intriguing story of Lacock Abbey in Wiltshire between the years 1685 and 1745; a behind-the-scenes view of very unusual domestic and noble interaction.

My work has taken more than two years of research and gathering together a wonderful group of professional and historic cooks, who have tested and advised, and brought the spirit of the old dishes back to life. They have cooked non-stop to produce these delicious and easy-to-prepare dishes, and they too have been an inspiration.

Mullicatunnie Soup.   Moretons

Put ½ a lb of butter in a Stew pan & about a dozen Onions
cut small – pass them well over the fire: then add to it
6 quarts of good Veal broth – cut up a couple of Chickens
as for a fricassee & put them in a Stewpan till quite
tender – then put into another Stew pan 6 Eschallots and
a few Turtle herbs – pass them over the fire – and add flour
sufficient to dry up the butter, & put to it four spoons
full of curry powder, & ½ an oz of Turmerie – pick out
your chicken & pour the broth into the other stewpan
& boil it all the while & squeeze in the juice of two
Lemons, season it to your palate – strain it to the
Chicken – and serve it up with Rice in a separate dish –.

For Walking Shoes.   Lord Ilchester & Lord Belmore.

1 Pint of oil of Linseed – 2 oz of Indian Rubber – a small
lump of bees wax. Melt all well together over a Stove &
when nearly cold rub it with a brush over your Shoes
(but not over the Soles of them) taking care to fill and
cover all the cracks & crevices particularly where the
Leathers join –. When the first coat is quite dry
which will be in 2 or 3 days put on another – & in a few
days more add another – It will keep out the wet of any
days Shooting –

The recipes cover three generations of the Talbot family, relatives of the Earl of Shrewsbury.

In all there are some twelve notebooks and manuscripts, written in several different hands. The only names identifiable were:

Lady Ivory (*née* Talbot) 1662-1720; her daughter Barbara Davenport (*née* Ivory) (m.1715, d.1748); and a granddaughter, Ann Talbot (1723-1752), who began writing the recipes aged 22, and who tragically died unmarried just seven years later. Ann Talbot's sister Martha Davenport (1720-1790) was most likely the elder Mrs Davenport, who has a receipt for 'A Toupee' dated 1772.

There are also important manuscripts by a Mary Davenport, with older handwriting and an illegible date, possibly 1692. She is probably Lady Ivory's cousin (b.1674), and possibly lived at Lacock as a relative/companion. She did not marry until she was 46, in the year 1720, which is notable because it was the year Lady Ivory died. She later married a second time.

In several cases, I have used the handwriting as my nearest guide to the probable date. Other original writers were either visitors (some of them royal guests) or other members of the Talbot family.

 To discover more about the secrets of Lacock Abbey scan here.

The Lacock Papers: Interesting and Unique

Lacock Abbey is different from most country houses, because the mistress of the house, Lady Ivory, started the family tradition of writing the recipes down. These are very early; a period of sixty years passed before Hannah Glasse became the first woman to publish a cookery book in England.

When Ann Talbot married Sir John Ivory in 1682, she appears to have flaunted the tradition of the kitchen and trespassed into the domain of the cook below stairs, pen, ink and paper poised - constantly disturbing the kitchen staff and demanding to know the ingredients and method of cooking of every single dish made.

Until about fifty years ago, the kitchen of a large country house was the domain of the cook and her kitchen maids, where even the scullery maids always remained at their washing up. The lady of the house held weekly meetings with her cook and housekeeper - above stairs.

It seems that the cook was regularly in a bad mood, as many of the recipes are far from complete, and often far from being palatable as a result! One of my tasks has been to fill in the missing details and recreate these dishes, testing and trying them out for your delight.

'Mullicatawnie Soup & For Walking Shoes', Lord Ilchester and Lord Belmore, 1745.

My book, *M'Lady's Book of Household Secrets* (The History Press, 2013) explains the duties of the mistress of the house, and the army of servants below stairs. The remedies and duties in the book are taken from the same Lacock Abbey Papers, and from my own family home, Castletown in County Kildare.

Other Sources

I was fascinated to find some of the ancient puddings at Lacock, especially the possetts and tanseys, were similar recipes to a favourite family dish from my own childhood. 'Old Irish Flummery' is included here, taken from my book *The Children of Castletown House* (The History Press, 2012).

Built by the family in 1722, Castletown is Ireland's first and finest Georgian house. Writing about my ancestors' adventures and intrigues, and how individual servants interacted with the Master and Mistress of the House, I discovered, for instance, that 'a great black porter' was first brewed in our village ... and that Guinness was the name of the family butler in the middle 1700s, some years before the Guinness brewery was founded in Dublin. He brewed his beer for the servants, as was the custom (upstairs drank wine). He was the father of Arthur Guinness, whose signature is on every bottle.

Our 'Black Porter Cake' recipe here has been created specially for you. It is made with Guinness, and was inspired by our family stories of the butler and his brew.

The second source of my own family recipes is in the handwritten 'Household Cookery Book' from an enchanting, pink-sandstone fairytale castle in Scotland. Thirlestane Castle, Lauder, my mother's birthplace, has 14in thick defensive walls, secret passages, and was a childhood delight.

What makes this cookery book interesting is its recipe for mixing authentic Indian curry powders, straight from the days of the Raj, which taste different from shop-bought varieties. They have been adapted here for use in the curry recipes we eat today.

Though these are of a later date, the mid-1800s, we are able to compare them with a curry dish from Lacock Abbey over 100 years earlier. And what a difference!

But what makes Lacock Abbey so very special is the discovery that the very modern habit of exchanging recipes after a lunch or dinner party was already alive and well amongst that handful of rare English families who took an interest in recipes in the seventeenth and eighteenth centuries.

 Scan here to find out more about Castletown House and the Conolly-Carew family.

 Scan here for some behind-the-scenes shots of Thirlestane Castle.

To pickle an old fat goosse

Cut it down the back and take out all the bones
then lard it very well with green Bakon & season
it with sault & 3 quarters of an ounce of peper
half an ounce of Ginger a quarter of an ounce of
Cloues & mace & a spoonfull of suger put it into
an earthen pott wth bay leaues at the botom one
whole onion & a clone of Garlick if you like it &
adde to all these a pint of white wine then couer the
pott close wth past & lett it bake wth great house
=hold bread or longer & then lett it lye in the pickle a
day or too & when you eat it scrape of the ffryce
& strain the pickle through a clean cloath & eat it
either with that pickle cold or with viniger

Royalty and Food Fashion

Lacock Abbey is a noble house with many royal connections.

It was built in 1232 as a nunnery by the Countess of Salisbury, whose husband was an illegitimate son of Henry ll. After the monasteries were sacked or closed by Henry Vlll in the mid-sixteenth century, Lacock Abbey was converted into a private house, and eventually passed down to the Talbots, the Earl of Shrewsbury's family.

Nowadays Lacock and the abbey are part of a National Trust picture-book village caught in an Olde England time warp, but with very modern attractions which led to the area being used as one of the Harry Potter film locations. Approximately 400 years ago, Lacock enjoyed a golden age, and a bridge built near the abbey diverted the main London-Bath road down the middle of Lacock High Street.

King Charles II visited the abbey, as did Queen Anne; they brought their endless retinues, the royal cooks, and their royal recipes. No stone was left unturned to welcome the royal guests. The records even state how meringues were served to the king or queen to show that the food was not poisoned.

During the reign of King Charles II, attempts were made to bring refinement in eating habits in the best company. The mid-seventeenth century was a time of change; table manners required learning the difficult art of eating with a knife and fork. A dagger was still acceptable as the knife, and the use of a fork turned out to be a tricky skill to learn. But using your fingers worked extremely well, so why bother? Meanwhile, noble ladies cajoled their stubborn husbands to practise the balancing act of getting stray bits into their mouths without any disasters down the front of a bejewelled waistcoat or a fancy ruff.

A Lasting Legacy

A wide selection of recipes has been included here to ensure you have a meal suitable for every occasion.

In order to help you choose which recipes to serve when, a selection of menus has also been included. Here you will find a king's menu, a prince's menu, a pauper's menu, a luncheon menu, a family menu, a favourite menu, a curry menu and a royal teatime menu, as well as healthy menus for the figure conscious.

Lady Ivory and her daughter and granddaughters took time and trouble to painstakingly write these recipes for their family, and, over 300 years later, they should be prized and enjoyed today and for years to come.

Conversion Tables

Weight

10g	½oz
20g	¾oz
25g	1oz
50g	2oz
75g	3oz
110g	4oz
150g	5oz
175g	6oz
200g	7oz
225g	8oz
250g	9oz
275g	10oz
350g	12oz
450g	16oz/1lb
700g	1½lbs
900g	2lbs
1.35kg	3lbs

Volume

5ml	1tsp	1tsp
15ml	1tbsp	1tbsp
60ml	2fl oz	4tbsp (¼ cup)
80ml	2¾fl oz	⅓ cup
125ml	4½fl oz	½ cup
160ml	5½ fl oz	⅔ cup
200ml	7fl oz	¾ cup
250ml	9fl oz	1 cup

Temperature

Heat	Gas Mark	F	C	Fan Oven
Very cool	1	275°	140°	120°
Cool	2	300°	150°	130°
Warm	3	325°	170°	150°
Moderate	4	350°	180°	160°
Fairly hot	5	375°	190°	170°
Fairly hot	6	400°	200°	180°
Hot	7	425°	220°	200°
Very hot	8	450°	230°	210°
Very hot	9	475°	240°	220°

Menus

The King's Menu

Smoked Trout Pâté Surprise

❦

Roast Sirloin of Beef (King Charles II)
or
Crown Roast of Lamb
or
Chicken, Cream & Leek Pie (Queen Elizabeth I)

❦

The King's Favourite Pudding (King Charles II)

The Prince's Menu

Spinach & Goats' Cheese Roulade

❦

Royal Venison Casserole (Prince John of Gaunt)

❦

Cherry Trifle with White Chocolate (Princess Victoria)
or
Swirl Cherry Cheesecake (Prince Edward, Duke of Windsor)

The Pauper's Menu

Scallop Loaf (or Oyster)

❦

Rabbit Pie

or

Great Lamb Pie

❦

Possett Brulée

The Family Menu

Lemon & Ginger Lamb Pasties

or

Meatballs in Tomato or Sweet Chilli Sauce

or

Roast Beef

❦

The King's Favourite Pudding

with

Flavoured Ice Creams

The Favourite Menu

Gruyère à la Crème Soup (served in a pumpkin)

Venison Casserole

Sweet Wine Ice Cream
or
The King's Favourite Pudding

The Curry Menu

Buttered Curried Chicken
with
Vegetable Side Dish
with
Poppadums & Mango Chutney
or
Curried Meatballs & Sauces

Orange with White Chocolate & Honeycomb
or
Sweet Wine Ice Cream

The Light Luncheon Menu

(All served with green beans &/or a large mixed salad with hot baguettes)

Smoked Haddock Chowder

or

Lemon & Ginger Lamb Pasties

or

Stuffed Vine Leaves

or

Scallop Loaf

or

Salmon and Oyster Pie

Sweet Wine Ice Cream

or

Swirl Cherry Cheesecake

The Healthy Menu (low calories)

Spinach, Goats' Cheese & Salmon Roulade

Fresh Salmon, Cod or Haddock with Mustard & Yoghurt Sauce

or

Stuffed Vine Leaves with Wild & Basmati Rice

The King's Favourite Pudding with Crumble or Filo Pastry

The Royal Teatime

Queen Anne liked both egg yolks and alcohol in her cup of tea.

The Duke of York's Cake, Buttered Teacake (The future King James II)
'Maids of Honour' Cakes (The Tudor court of Queen Elizabeth I)
'Kisses', tiny Meringues Filled with Cream (Queen Henrietta Maria)
Raspberry Cakes (Lacock Abbey at the time of King Charles II)

Part of the contents
of Lady Ivory's
Recipe Book.

Starters

Spinach, Goats' Cheese & Salmon Roulade

Spinach and goats' cheese are perfect partners and make a healthy starter. This recipe was inspired by Ann Talbot's recipe for 'Spinage Tart'.

Serves 4-6

Ingredients

ROULADE

85g (3 cups) SPINACH LEAVES
2 GARLIC CLOVES, peeled and chopped
2tbsp CRÈME FRAÎCHE
4 EGGS, separated

FILLING

150g (½ cup) SMOKED SALMON, chopped
250g (9oz) RICOTTA
150g (5oz) GOATS' CHEESE, cubed
1 RED PEPPER, grilled, skinned and chopped
1tbsp FRESH PARSLEY, chopped, plus a few sprigs of parsley for decoration
1tbsp FRESH BASIL, chopped
SEA SALT and fresh ground BLACK PEPPER, to taste

Method

1. Preheat the oven to 200°C (400°F).
2. Line a 38cm×25cm (15inx10in) Swiss roll tin with baking parchment.
3. Mix the spinach and garlic in a food processor or blender to a rough purée.
4. Take out the mixture and place into a mixing bowl with the crème fraîche and egg yolks. Whisk and season well.
5. Whisk the egg whites separately to soft peaks, and fold into the spinach mixture.
6. Spread the roulade mix fairly thinly onto the prepared Swiss roll tin, and bake for 10 minutes until golden and firm.
7. Remove from the oven and leave to cool.

TO MAKE THE FILLING

1. Mix the smoked salmon, ricotta, goats' cheese, red pepper, and herbs together. Season well.

2. When the roulade is cold, invert it onto a clean tea towel or on to fresh baking parchment.

3. Peel away the old baking parchment from the roulade.

4. With the short side facing you, spread the goats' cheese filling from the edge facing you, spreading it over the roulade - leaving a 2cm (1in) gap on the other 3 edges.

5. Gently roll up, and place on a serving dish with the seam side down.

Serving

Serve cold on a white plate for dramatic effect, with lemon wedges, a few green salad leaves, and a separate tomato vinaigrette dressing.

This recipe can also be done with fresh salmon, smoked haddock, or mushrooms.

Original Recipe

To Make a Spinage Tart

Take a quart of cream and boyle it and beat 8 eggs and put into it but have a care it doge not curdle put in a nutmeg grated and some sugar then take the marrow of 2 bones and cut it small and put it in with half a pound of currans then take a good handfull of spinage well wash't and cut it small and just scald it and mix it altogether then rowle a sheet of past and put on the bottom of yr dish and power it in with some candy'd orange and lemon peel then put some crose-bars of past over it so bake it and scrape some sugar over it

'To Make a Spinage Tart' by Ann Talbot, Lacock Abbey, 1745.

Spinach or Watercress Mousse

Ann Talbot's use of spinach as a first course inspired this alternative spinach starter.

Serves
4-6

Ingredients

250g (2 cups) CREAM CHEESE
150ml (⅔ cup) MAYONNAISE
1 sachet GELATINE
150ml (⅔ cup) CHICKEN STOCK
   (warmed through)
3 handfuls of SPINACH LEAVES,
   washed OR 4 bunches of
   WATERCRESS with stalks
A few drops of TABASCO, to taste
SALT and PEPPER to taste
150ml (⅔ cup) DOUBLE
   (HEAVY) CREAM

FOR THE DECORATION

Each helping has a few PRAWNS
   (JUMBO SHRIMP) and a small
   twist of SMOKED SALMON

Method

1. In a bowl, beat the cream cheese until smooth.
2. Stir in the mayonnaise and set aside.
3. Dissolve the gelatine in the warmed chicken stock and leave to cool.
4. In a blender or food processor, purée the spinach (or watercress), including the stalks.
5. Add the chicken and gelatine stock along with the tabasco and salt and pepper to taste.
6. In a separate bowl, whisk the cream into soft peaks.
7. Add the cream to the cream cheese and mayonnaise mixture using a metal spoon.
8. With the same method, add the spinach (or watercress) purée.
9. Pour or spoon the mixture into individual ramekin dishes (or one large dish) and leave until set.

Serving

Serve with a sprig of watercress as decoration, accompanied by a few prawns (jumbo shrimp) and a small twist of smoked salmon to make this a special dish. Serve with a hot baguette, cut into approximately 4cm (1½in) slices.

Gruyère à la
Crème Soup
Served in a
Pumpkin

This is a modern-day version of the 'White Soop' recipe recorded by Ann Talbot in 1745. If served in a pumpkin it is guaranteed to excite.

Serves
8-10

V

Ingredients

1 PUMPKIN weighing 3-4kg (6-8½lbs)
100-150g (1-1⅓ cup) GRUYÈRE
   CHEESE, grated
Enough very fresh SINGLE
   (LIGHT) CREAM to fill the last
   quarter of the pumpkin
SALT and freshly ground
   BLACK PEPPER, to taste
GRATED NUTMEG
200-250g (3-4 cup) SMALL CROÛTONS

Method

1. Preheat the oven to 165°C (320°F).
2. Cut off the top of the pumpkin so that it will make a tureen. Keep the lid.
3. Carefully scoop out the seeds and stringy fibres with a spoon.
4. Put alternate layers of croûtons and Gruyère cheese into the pumpkin until it is three-quarters full.
5. Season the cream with salt, pepper and grated nutmeg, and pour into the pumpkin until it is full. Cover with the lid and cook in the oven for 2 hours.
6. Stir gently with a ladle from time to time to obtain a smooth consistency, taking care to replace the lid.

Serving

Carry the covered pumpkin to the table. Pour a ladle
of soup into each heated bowl, adding some croûtons
sprinkled with cheese and a piece of the pumpkin flesh
scooped out with a spoon.

the white soop of m.rs Mytton   m.rs Eyers

Take 6 or 8 pound of veel & 2 or 3 pound of
mutton put a sufficient quantity of water some
pepper clower & mace & a small oynion let it boyle
very well & have half a pound of sweet almonds beat
small & w.th the broath let it pass through a sive
till it is all mixt & a little before you serve it
up put in near a pint of good cream & put in the
dish some poached eggs & the crust of french
role

'The White Soop of Mrs Myltons - Mrs Eyers', Ann Talbot, Lacock Abbey, 1745.

Scallop (or Oyster) Loaves

Scallop Loaves provide an interesting and popular light luncheon. Oysters can be used instead, but they do not suit everyone and are more expensive (8 scallops are half the price of 10-12 oysters). A similar recipe for 'Oyster Loaves' was recorded by Lady Ivory of Lacock Abbey in 1685.

Serves
4

Ingredients

4 SMALL COTTAGE LOAVES
12 walnut-sized knobs of BUTTER
4 SMALL ONION
4 small sprigs of THYME
4tbsp of FISH STOCK
6-8tsp of WATER
8 SCALLOPS (fresh on the day), sliced
8 EGG YOLKS

Method

1. Cut the top off the loaves and hollow them out.
2. Gently melt four knobs of butter.
3. Brush the crusts with the melted butter and keep them warm in a low oven.
4. To make the stock/water, sauté the onions with the thyme, mix in the fish stock and add the water.
5. Add sliced scallops to the stock/water for a very short time until just cooked.
6. To thicken the stock, beat 4 egg yolks and add some of the stock/water to it.
7. SLOWLY return this to the pan with the rest of the scallop mixture, so as not to curdle, with 4 more walnut-sized knobs of butter.
8. When thickened, put mixture into the warm loaves.
9. Add the other melted walnut-sized knobs of butter on the top.

10. Then pour the other beaten egg yolks over the top.
11. Place the loaves under a moderately hot grill and watch carefully until egg firms and begins to brown (do not let it burn).

Serve immediately.

Original Recipe

'Oyster Loaves', Lady Ivory, Lacock Abbey, 1685.

Smoked Haddock Chowder

Thick cod or haddock soups were popular on 'fish days' from the Middle Ages onwards. This creamy Chowder is slightly thicker than the older variants and has been given a sweetcorn accompaniment.

Serves
6

Ingredients

1 BAY LEAF

1,100ml (4¼ cup) FULL-CREAM MILK

1 LARGE ONION, cut in half

2 CLOVES, 1 pressed into
each half of onion

2 sticks of CELERY, cut
into 6-8 thin slices

1 whole piece SMOKED HADDOCK

500g (1lbs) POTATOES

Optional - SMALL TIN OF
SWEETCORN, drained

Bunch of PARSLEY

Method

1. Place bay leaf, milk, onion, cloves, celery and haddock in a large lidded frying pan.

2. Replace the lid, bring to simmering point, and cook on the hob for approximately 10 minutes.

3. In the meantime, chop the parsley and set aside. Dice and chop the potatoes into small 1¼cm (½in) squares.

4. Remove the fish from the mixture when it is cooked and leave it to get cold.

5. Place the diced potatoes into the chowder milk, and keep cooking until the potatoes are just soft (not overdone).

6. With a slotted spoon remove approximately half of the potatoes and vegetables, and place them in a mixer with approximately half of the chowder milk.

7. Mix quickly and put it back into the frying pan with the other milk. Stir it well to thicken the mixture.

8. When the haddock is cold enough, flake the fish into the chowder, and add the well-drained sweetcorn (if you take that option).

9. Take time to heat thoroughly, but gently.

Serving

Serve in soup
bowls with a
good sprinkling
of parsley on
top. Serve with
a hot loaf of
sourdough bread.

'Crayfish and Pottage' recipe from Lord Lund, Lacock Abbey, 1725.

Smoked Trout Pâté Surprise

Every grand country house had manmade lakes for their fresh-water fish - usually constructed with a stream running through and safety stop-locks at either end to prevent the fish escaping. This meant trout was often on the menu.

Serves
6-8

Ingredients

125g (1 cup) CREAM CHEESE
2-3tsp (heaped) HORSERADISH
2 LEMONS
1 bunch FRESH CHIVES,
   finely chopped
SEA SALT and GROUND
   PEPPER, to taste
125g (½ fillet) hot SMOKED TROUT,
   with skin and any bones removed
175g (1 cup) RED OR BELUGA CAVIAR
RAPESEED OIL

Method

1. Put the cream cheese into a mixing bowl with the horseradish, the zest of 1 lemon and the juice from ½ the lemon, and mix together.

2. Add most of the chopped chives and mix well. Taste and add a little salt and pepper if needed.

3. Add more horseradish and/or lemon juice to taste to give it a kick.

4. Fold the deboned trout (in small chunks) into the mixture using a thick knife or spatula. Be careful not break up the pieces of smoked trout.

5. Select six or eight ramekin dishes or cups or glasses and three-quarters fill each cup with the mixture.

6. Then add a teaspoon of caviar in the middle, and top up with more pâté mixture.

7. Drizzle over a little rapeseed oil and sprinkle with a few more finely chopped chives.

8. Cover with cling film and keep in the fridge to settle for at least a couple of hours.

Serving

Serve with grated lemon zest on the top of each ramekin along with lemon wedges and with a plate of wholemeal toast 'soldiers' served under napkins to keep hot.

Light
Lunches

Chicken, Cream & Leek Pie

This was a favourite of Queen Elizabeth I. The name of this recipe changed through the decades (as did the spelling): in 1580 it was called 'Chekyns in Sauce' and by 1685, it was known as 'Frigesey of Chicken'.

Serves 6-8

Ingredients

FILLING

1 CHICKEN (about 1.5kg (3¼lbs))
2 CELERY STICKS, chopped
1 CARROT, chopped
2 ONIONS, finely chopped
6-8 sprigs FRESH TARRAGON
SALT and PEPPER, to taste
1tbsp OLIVE OIL
Knob of BUTTER
2 LEEKS, finely sliced
150ml (⅔ cup) SWEET WHITE WINE
2tbsp PLAIN (SOFT) FLOUR
150ml (⅔ cup) DOUBLE (HEAVY) CREAM
    OR CRÈME FRAÎCHE
Zest of ½ a LEMON

PASTRY

600g (1¼lbs) RICH SHORTCRUST PASTRY
1 EGG, beaten, for glazing

Recommended Wines

Grüner Veltliner
Chablis (1st Cru or Grand Cru)
Viognier

'The Court uses the whole chicken. It is chopped up for the others.'

- A quote from the Elizabethan court of 1580, cited in *Court Favourites* by Elizabeth Craig

Method

1. Preheat the oven to 200°C (400°F) and place a baking tray into the oven to heat.
2. Place the chicken in a deep pan along with the carrot, celery and half the onions. Place 4 sprigs of tarragon on the top, season with salt and pepper, and cover with cold water.
3. Bring to the boil and simmer for 45 minutes, or until the chicken is cooked.
4. Lift out the chicken and set aside to cool.
5. Simmer the chicken stock for 30 minutes, reducing the liquid by half.
6. In a large frying pan, heat the oil and butter gently, add the remaining onions and the leeks, and cook until soft.
7. Turn up the heat, add the wine, and cook for 4 minutes, reducing by half.
8. Add the flour and stir for a minute, making sure there are no lumps.
9. Now stir in the cream (or the crème fraîche), 150ml (⅔ cup) of the reduced chicken stock, and the lemon zest. Season to taste and allow to cool.
10. Chop or shred the meat from the cooked chicken, discarding the skin and bones.
11. Add the chicken meat along with the remaining chopped tarragon to the leeks and cream mixture, and stir together.
12. Roll out ⅔ of the pastry on a floured surface.
13. Line a 23cm (9in) round pie dish or tin with the rolled-out pastry.
14. Fill with the chicken mixture, and brush the edges of the pastry case with beaten egg.
15. Now roll out the remaining pastry to make a lid. Lay it over the filling, crimp the edges to seal, and trim away the excess.
16. Brush with the beaten egg, place on the baking tray and cook for 45 minutes.

Original Recipe

'To Make a Frigesey of Chicken', Lady Ivory, Lacock Abbey, 1685.

Salmon & Oyster Pie

Fish pie was a popular dish. This is a version of Fish Pottage which has been turned into a pie with a modern Parmesan topping.

Serves
4-6

Original Recipe

To season a salmon pye

when you have made yr pye put in a good piece of salmon & 2 quarts of oysters & 2 quarts of shrimps & prawns a quarter of an ounce of whole mace some 2 nutmegs quartered 4 Anchovies half an ounce of beaten ginger salt & 3 pound of butter so lid yt so bake it well & eat it cold

'To Season a Salmon Pye', Ann Talbot, Lacock Abbey, 1745.

Ingredients

FILLING

120ml (½ cup) WHITE WINE
1 tin ANCHOVIES IN OIL
   (50g (2oz) size)
A pinch of GRANULATED SUGAR
480g (1¼ fillets) SALMON
1 tin SMOKED OYSTERS IN OIL
   (85g size (½ cup)) OR ½ packet
   of KIPPER FILLETS
200g (¾ cup) PRAWNS
   (JUMBO SHRIMP)
50g (¼ cup) BUTTER
2.5cm (1in) FRESH GINGER, crushed
2-3 pieces WHOLE MACE
1 NUTMEG broken into small pieces
½ FISH STOCK CUBE
30g (¼ cup) PLAIN (SOFT) FLOUR

TOPPING

2 large SWEET POTATOES,
   peeled and diced
2tbsp BUTTER
SALT and PEPPER, to taste
1 big handful of grated
   PARMESAN CHEESE

Recommended Wines

Gewürztraminer

Method

TO MAKE THE TOPPING

1. Steam the diced sweet potatoes until tender (or you can boil them in salted water).
2. Drain well, add butter and seasoning and mash well.
3. Keep the topping until the salmon pie is ready.

TO MAKE THE FILLING

1. Preheat the oven to 200°C (400°F).
2. Pour the wine into small bowl.
3. Chop the anchovies into small pieces (discarding the oil) and add them to the wine.
4. Heat an empty heavy saucepan and pour the wine and anchovies into the hot pan, cooking off the alcohol.
5. Stir in a pinch of sugar and keep stirring on a gentle boil to reduce the liquid slightly.
6. Add the salmon and lightly poach.
7. Remove the salmon and break it up gently, placing it in a pie dish.
8. Remove some of the anchovies and add them to the dish.
9. Add the oysters or kippers and prawns (jumbo shrimp).
10. Make a white sauce with melted butter, fish liquor left in the saucepan (including the rest of the anchovies), ginger, mace, nutmeg, fish stock cube and flour.
11. Pour the sauce over the fish.
12. Spoon the topping unevenly over the pie, sprinkle the Parmesan over the top, and put the pie in the oven.
13. Cook until the topping is golden and crisp.
14. It takes approximately 20 minutes, but you must watch your oven, so it does not overcook.

Fish Sauce à la Lacock

This sauce is delicious with haddock, cod, or carp and is similar to the 1745 'Carp Sauce' recipe by Lord Thomas Lyttleton of Lacock Abbey.

Serves
4

Ingredients

40g (¼ cup) BUTTER
2 SHALLOTS, finely chopped
6 ANCHOVIES, in oil
25g (¼ cup) PLAIN (SOFT) FLOUR
400ml (1¼ cup) FISH STOCK
1tbsp FRESH LEMON JUICE
1tsp (heaped) HORSERADISH,
    grated fresh, or sauce from
    a jar - not creamed
½tsp GROUND MACE
½tsp GROUND NUTMEG

Method

1. Melt the butter in a small pan, add the shallots and anchovies and cook very gently until the onion is soft and the anchovies begin to melt.
2. Stir in the flour and cook for 1-2 minutes, stirring continuously.
3. Gradually whisk in the fish stock and stir until thickened.
4. Add lemon juice, horseradish, mace and nutmeg to taste.

Original Recipe

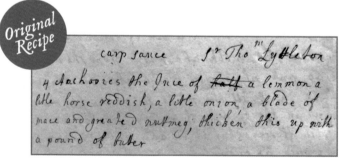

carp sauce   Sr Thomas Lyttleton

4 Anchovies the Juice of ~~half~~ a lemmon a litle horse reddish, a little onion, a blade of mace and greated nutmeg, thicken this up with a pound of buter

'Carp Sauce', Lord Thomas Lyttleton, Lacock Abbey, 1745.

Mustard & Yoghurt Sauce

A healthy alternative to Fish Sauce à la Lacock.

Serves 4   V

Ingredients

60g (¼ cup) LOW-FAT PLAIN
   GREEK YOGHURT
1tbsp DIJON MUSTARD
60ml (¼ cup) fresh LEMON JUICE
2tbsp fresh CHOPPED CHIVES

Method

1. Combine the yoghurt, Dijon mustard, lemon juice and chives.
2. Whisk to mix well.
3. Pour over cooked salmon, cod or haddock.

Rabbit Pie

Eating rabbit is no longer fashionable but once it was staple fare for both the upper and lower classes.

Serves
4-6

Ingredients

SUET CRUST PASTRY

350g (3 cup) SELF-RAISING FLOUR
175g (1½ cup) SUET, shredded
½tsp SALT and BLACK PEPPER, to taste
Approx. 100-150ml (⅓-⅔cup) WATER

Original Recipe

'How to Roast Rabbitts', Lady Ivory, Lacock Abbey, 1685.

FILLING

1 RABBIT - approximately 1.35kg
    (3lbs) - from the butcher
275ml (2 cup) CIDER
425ml (1⅞ cup) CHICKEN STOCK
225g (8oz) UNSMOKED STREAKY
    BACON in a whole piece (unsliced)
2 medium ONIONS, chopped up small
1 medium COOKING APPLE,
    peeled and sliced
¼ NUTMEG, grated
FRESH ROSEMARY, a good sprinkle
1 whole CLOVE
1 BAY LEAF
225g (1 cup) chopped PRUNES
    (stones removed)
40g (⅓ cup) PLAIN (SOFT) FLOUR
50g (¼ cup) BUTTER

Method

TO MAKE THE FILLING

1. Cut the rabbit into joints and wash them, discarding the ribs.
2. Place them in a large dish and cover with the cider and stock.
3. Cover and marinate for 24 hours.
4. Carefully transfer the rabbit and its marinade into a deep, lidded saucepan.
5. Remove the rind from the bacon piece, and cut it up into rough 2.5cm (1in) squares.
6. Add the bacon squares, chopped onions, and sliced cooking apple to the rabbit marinade.
7. Add the spices/herbs and season lightly. Bring to the boil and skim off any scum from the top.
8. Put the lid on the saucepan, turn the heat down, and simmer gently for about 1 hour.
9. When the meat is tender, using a slotted spoon, transfer the rabbit joints, onion, apple, and bacon into a pie dish, and cover with the chopped prunes.
10. In order to thicken the marinade left in the saucepan, mix the flour and butter into a smooth paste, and add it to the stock in the saucepan, stirring well until the paste melts and the sauce thickens.
11. Bring the sauce to a gentle rolling boil and then pour it over the rabbit.

TO MAKE THE SUET CRUST PASTRY

1. Preheat the oven to 180°C (350°F).
2. Mix the flour, suet salt, and pepper together.
3. Add enough cold water for a soft dough that leaves the bowl cleanly.
4. Roll the dough into a shape 2.5cm (1in) wider than the top of the pie dish.
5. Cut a 2.5cm (1in) strip all round to fit around the edge of the pie dish and press it into place.
6. Add the pie filling, then dampen the rim of the pastry, place the pastry lid on the top and seal the edges.
7. Decorate as you like and make a hole for steam to escape.
8. Bake for 35 minutes or until golden brown.

Recommended Wines

Chianti
Viognier
Rioja

Stuffed Vine Leaves

It is interesting to find this dish at Lacock Abbey - does it mean they grew vines in the 1600s? The original recipe used veal but a half-and-half mixture of minced beef and pork has more flavour.

Serves
4-6

Ingredients

225g (8oz) PORK
225g (8oz) BEEF
75g (½ cup) RED ONION,
    blanched (sweated)
20 ANCHOVIES, chopped
1tbsp SUET
2tbsp OREGANO
About 50 VINE LEAVES,
    fresh, or packed in brine
    (for preparation, see Notes)

COOKING LIQUOR

120ml (½ cup) WHITE WINE
120ml (½ cup) WHITE WINE VINEGAR
5 whole ANCHOVIES
WATER to cover, as required

Method

1. Put the pork and beef in a food processor, add the blanched onion, anchovies, suet and oregano, and blend in a food processor to obtain a fine mixture.

2. Take handfuls of the mixture and roll into sausage shapes, about 1cm (½in) in diameter and about 5cm (2in) long. Wrap the sausages in cling film, roll on a flat surface to maintain their roundness, and twist the ends up tightly.

3. Place the wrapped sausages in an ovenproof dish, and put them in a freezer for about 40 minutes only.

4. Remove the dish from the freezer, take one sausage and cut it into three pieces.

5. Take three leaves and lay them vein side up on a flat surface. Place a piece of the sausage on the leaves and roll up the vine leaves, tucking in the sides as you roll.

6. Place in the ovenproof dish, seam-side down. Continue cutting and rolling until all the mixture and leaves are finished. Place 5 whole anchovies on the top of the rolls.

'Stuffed Vine Leaves', Lady Ivory, Lacock Abbey, 1685.

7. Pour a mixture of 4 tablespoons of wine and 4 tablespoons of white wine vinegar over the dish, and add water to just cover the food.

8. Using another suitable ovenproof dish, weigh down the leaves and anchovies.

9. Bake at 180°C (350°F) for 40 minutes.

Serving

Serve in a bed of basmati and wild rice with batons of brightly coloured vegetables.

Recommended Wines

Beaujolais

Fiano

Notes

1. If anchovies are too salty for your taste, soak them in milk to reduce the salt content.

2. Preserved vine leaves are difficult to separate. Place the leaves in a suitable bowl and pour boiling water over them. Then use a wooden spoon to gently separate the leaves. Increase the depth of boiling water to about 5cm (2in), and leave for 20 minutes. Drain the leaves well in a colander, then cut off and discard the stalks. Cover and chill the leaves for about an hour before using them.

Meatballs

Lady Ivory recorded a recipe for 'Forced Meat Balls' in 1685 which used the same forced-meat mixture as the Stuffed Vine Leaves. This dish has been updated to give a bit of extra taste and bite.

Serves 4-6

Ingredients

225g (8oz) MINCED BEEF
225g (8oz) MINCED PORK (add a
    little suet if the meat is very lean)
Ground BLACK PEPPER
    and SALT, to taste
1 dessertspoon of
    GRATED ORANGE PEEL
1tbsp FRESH THYME, finely chopped
1 slice DRY WHITE BREAD
2 EGGS, beaten

SAUCE

240ml (1 cup) VEGETABLE STOCK
2tbsp CORNFLOUR (CORNSTARCH)
1 tbsp of MADEIRA WINE
A squeeze of LEMON JUICE

Method

1. Gradually add the beaten eggs to all
   the other ingredients to bind and shape
   them together into 12 meatballs.

2. Fry gently, turning frequently until golden
   brown and cooked through. Remove the
   meatballs from the pan and keep warm.

TO MAKE THE SAUCE

1. Mix 1 tablespoon of the vegetable stock
   with the cornflour (cornstarch), and pour
   this into the rest of the stock.

2. Stir continuously, heat and thicken, then add 1
   tablespoon of Madeira and a squeeze of lemon juice.

3. Pour into the same pan in which the meatballs
   were cooked, and stir until the sauce has
   thickened. Pour over the meatballs.

ALTERNATIVE SAUCES

Fresh tomato sauce — Onion, garlic, fresh and puréed tomatoes, sugar, basil and Parmesan.

Light curry sauce — 1 tablespoon curry powder, flour, butter; salt and 1 cup coconut milk.

You can also use Thai sweet chilli sauce, if you prefer.

Recommended Wines

Bergerac

Verdejo

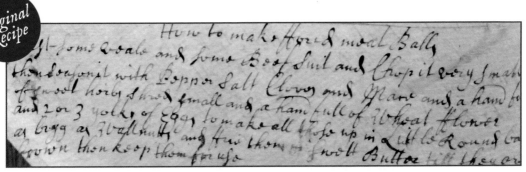

Original Recipe

'How to make Forced Meat Balls', Lady Ivory, Lacock Abbey, 1685.

Main Courses

The main course is a feature in all old cookery books. Main course dishes have changed little over the years and needed little adaptation for the modern palate. Steaks were very common and were almost always marinated.

Marinades

It was common in the seventeenth-century tradition to marinate nearly all meats for 24 hours. This improves the meat's texture and enriches every dish. Sugar also played an important part in historic cooking. One teaspoon of sugar added to red cooking wine in a marinade or gravy, draws out the acidity, and behaves like best red claret. Some marinades are contained within the recipes but here are a few you can use to improve your old favourite recipes.

Nettle (Chicken)

3 handfuls of NETTLE TOPS
2tbsp CIDER VINEGAR
250ml (1 cup) WHITE WINE
   (medium dry Italian)
1 SHALLOT, finely chopped
2tsp chopped CORIANDER
1 LEMON, juice and zest
2tbp OLIVE OIL

Ginger Wine (Pork)

250ml (1 cup) GINGER WINE
50ml (¼ cup) SOY SAUCE
2tbsp BROWN SUGAR
10 WILD GARLIC LEAVES
50ml (¼ cup) OLIVE OIL
30g (¼ cup) SPRING ONIONS,
   finely chopped

BBQ

250ml (1 cup) RED WINE
   (Côtes du Rhône)
50ml (¼ cup) BALSAMIC VINEGAR
2tsp CHOPPED BASIL
½tsp grated GINGER
1 clove GARLIC, crushed
Small sprig ROSEMARY
1 RED CHILLI, seeded and
   finely chopped
Ground BLACK PEPPER
Blend to a coarse purée

Venison

250ml (1 cup) RED WINE (Merlot)
2tbsp RED WINE VINEGAR
2 LEEKS, thinly sliced
1 BAY LEAF
4 JUNIPER BERRIES, lightly crushed
3tbsp OIL
1 clove GARLIC, crushed
½tsp crushed PEPPERCORNS
2tsp DIJON MUSTARD

Lamb

250ml (1 cup) OIL
250ml (1 cup) WHITE WINE (Muscadet)
4 CLOVES
1 ONION, sliced
1 CARROT, sliced
1 stick CELERY, sliced
1tsp chopped TARRAGON
2 ANCHOVIES, chopped

Beef

250ml (1 cup) RED WINE (Italian)
½ LEMON, sliced
1 BAY LEAF
¼tsp chopped TARRAGON
¼tsp chopped CHIVES
1 pinch of THYME
1 clove GARLIC, chopped
2tbsp OLIVE OIL

Roast Beef

Roast beef has been a favourite for generations. This recipe is based on Ann Talbot's 1745 recipe 'To bake a rump of beafe'.

Serves 8

Ingredients

2-2.5kg (4-5¼lbs) ROLLED RUMP (OR SIRLOIN) JOINT OF BEEF (ask the butcher to supply the BEEF BONES separately)
SALT and PEPPER, to taste
600ml (2½ cup) RED WINE
1.1 litres (4⅔ cup) GUINNESS
12 ANCHOVIES, chopped
2 handfuls CAPERS, minced small
2 medium ONIONS, chopped
2 cloves GARLIC, crushed
SWEET HERBS (bouquet garni)
1 NUTMEG, cut in pieces

Method

1. Preheat the oven to 170°C (325°F).
2. Put all the ingredients in a large baking dish, making sure the wine and beer cover the meat.
3. Put the bones on the top and cover with a lid (or a double thickness of foil).
4. Leave in the oven at 170°C (325°F) for 2 hours; and turn down to 140°C (275°F) for a further 4 hours.
5. Carefully remove the joint and keep warm.
6. Reduce the juices by boiling until half the quantity is left - this thickens and concentrates the flavour of the gravy.
7. If thicker gravy is preferred, carefully mix in a little sieved flour and stir until dissolved.

Recommended Wines

Rioja Gran Reserva
Cabernet Sauvignon

> 'Our Second Charles of fame facete,
> On lion of beef did dine.
> He held his sword, pleased, o'er the meat:
> "Arise, the famed Sir Lion".'
>
> - *Court Favourites*

Original Recipe

To bake a rump of beafe & some bone it and feafon it with paper and falt and take a pint of Claret and a quart of Ale or strong stale beer 12 anchovies 2 handfalls of Cappers mince't fmall fax onyions and a clove or 2 of garlick a fagott of sweet heorbs and a nutmeg cut in peices put these in a pan together and put the bones upon it then cover it with course past and lett it bake 6 or 7 hours

'To bake a rump of beafe', Ann Talbot, Lacock Abbey, 1745.

Marinated Sirloin (or Rump) Steak

The perfect steaks are 4cm (1½in) thick. Allow half a rump or sirloin steak per person. They need to rest for 5-7 minutes after cooking before serving, so transfer the steaks to a cutting board and place them under a large tented piece of foil. Use the 5-7 minutes to make the sauce.

Serves 6-8

Ingredients

3-4 rump or sirloin STEAKS

MARINADE

RED WINE (inexpensive), to cover
1 heaped tbsp SUGAR
2 cloves GARLIC, crushed
1tsp FRESH BASIL
1tsp FRESH THYME
1tsp FRESH SAGE

SAUCE

10g (1tbsp) BUTTER
½ BEEF STOCK CUBE
1tbsp PLAIN (SOFT) FLOUR
4tbsp REDCURRANT JELLY
SALT and PEPPER, to taste

Method

1. Cover the steaks in the marinade for 24 hours.

TO MAKE THE SAUCE

1. Remove the steaks from the marinade and set aside.
2. Strain the marinade to take out the bits.
3. Melt the butter and add ½ a beef stock cube.
4. Mix in the flour.
5. Add the strained marinade and bring to the boil.
6. Add the redcurrant jelly and stir.
7. Heat for 5 minutes or until liquid has thickened.
8. Add salt and pepper if necessary and keep hot.
9. Fry the steaks in oil for approximately 4 minutes each side.

Serving

Serve each steak cut into 4-6 long slices in a fan shape to reveal the pink centre (but do not cut all the way through). Pour the sauce over the top.

Recommended Wines

Bordeaux Claret
Malbec

Alternative Sauces

Béarnaise sauce is thought to have been named in honour of Henry IV of France, who was born in Béarn.

Béarnaise Sauce

Ingredients	Method
4 SHALLOTS	1. Peel and chop the shallots.
70ml (⅓ cup) MALT VINEGAR	2. Place in a saucepan with the vinegars and crushed peppercorns.
70ml (⅓ cup) TARRAGON VINEGAR	
6 PEPPERCORNS	3. Bring to the boil and boil until the vinegar is reduced to ⅓ of its original quantity.
140ml (⅔ cup) BÉCHAMEL SAUCE	
4 EGG YOLKS	4. Strain and add to the béchamel sauce, stirring constantly.
75g (⅓ cup) BUTTER	
	5. Stir until hot, then remove from the heat and stir in the egg yolks, one at a time, with a wooden spoon.
	6. Return to a low heat and stir until thickened, but do not allow the sauce to boil.
	7. Add the butter, bit by bit, allowing each piece to melt before putting in the next.

Blue Cheese Butter (made in advance)

Ingredients	Method

Ingredients

450g (1¼ cup) UNSALTED BUTTER
(room temperature)
175g (6oz) BLUE CHEESE

Method

1. In a large bowl, mash the butter with a potato masher, or knead it to get it soft enough to add the cheese.
2. Add the blue cheese and continue mashing the butter until it is fully mixed.
3. Place a piece of cling film (about 30cm (1ft) square) on top of the work surface.
4. Scoop the butter mixture into the middle of the cling film.
5. Roll the butter into a cylinder-shape inside the plastic.
6. Tie both ends of the film into a knot.
7. Chill or freeze until needed.

Serving

Serve thick slices of the Blue Cheese Butter on top of hot, freshly cooked steaks as you serve them up.

Small Barrel Fillet Steak

As long as it is marinated, this is still the best way to eat a modern steak - cut small, deep, and round or square in shape.

Serves
6-8

Ingredients

6-8 STEAKS, 4cm (1½in) thick

MARINADE

300ml (1¼ cup) OLIVE OIL
300ml (1¼ cup) BALSAMIC VINEGAR
2 cloves of GARLIC, crushed
1tsp FRESH BASIL
1tsp FRESH THYME
1tsp SAGE
SALT and PEPPER, to taste

SAUCE

10g (1tbsp) BUTTER
½ BEEF STOCK CUBE
1tbsp PLAIN (SOFT) FLOUR
300ml (1¼ cup) CREAM
1tbsp APRICOT JAM
1tbsp DIJON MUSTARD

Method

1. Cover the steaks in the marinade for 24 hours.

TO MAKE THE SAUCE

1. Remove the meat from the marinade and set aside.
2. Remove the excess olive oil from the top of the marinade liquid.
3. Strain the marinade.
4. Melt 10g butter and stir in ½ a beef stock cube and the flour.
5. Add the strained marinade.
6. When heated through, add the cream, apricot jam and Dijon mustard.
7. Mix together and heat for several minutes, stirring continuously.
8. Add salt and pepper if required, along with a little water to obtain correct pouring consistency.
9. Keep the sauce hot.
10. Fry the steaks in a skillet for approximately 4 minutes,

browning top and bottom well. Cut a small slice out of each steak to check that they are pink in the middle, but cooked enough.

11. Serve with the sauce over each steak.

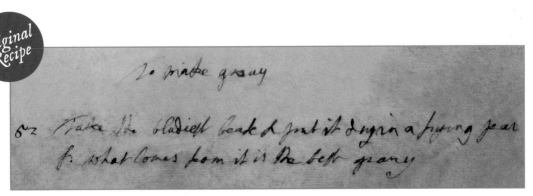

'To make gravy', Ann Talbot, Lacock Abbey, 1745.

Royal Venison Casserole with Berries

This recipe originally called for Prince John of Gaunt's venison, hunted in his deer park in the Forest of Knaresborough, *c.* 1370.

Serves 6-8

Ingredients

1kg (2¼lbs) diced VENISON STEAK
Large knob of BUTTER OR DRIPPING
6-10 SHALLOTS OR 3 finely
    chopped cloves of GARLIC
1½tbsp PLAIN (SOFT) FLOUR
200ml (¾ cup) CRANBERRY JUICE
3 large handfuls of CRANBERRIES
OLIVE OIL as necessary

MARINADE

RED WINE
1tsp SUGAR
1 handful of FRESH ROSEMARY,
    crushed in the hand

Method

1. Marinate the steak in red wine (to cover), sugar, and fresh rosemary for 24 hours.
2. Preheat the oven to 180°C (350°F).
3. Melt the butter/dripping in pan, add 6-10 whole shallots or chopped garlic, and cook until brown.
4. Remove the shallots or garlic and place in a dish.
5. Remove the venison from its marinade, pat dry with kitchen paper and brown in the pan. Then add it to the dish with shallots.
6. Add a little flour to the fat and juice left in the pan, and cook gently, stirring continuously.
7. Then add cranberry juice (or blackberry or similar juice), bring to the boil and cook.
8. Then add 3 large handfuls of cranberries (or blackberries etc.) and add to venison.
9. Add more juice and a little olive oil if necessary (to make sure the venison is covered).
10. Put in the oven for 45 minutes, reduce heat to 150°C (300°F) and cook for a further 30 minutes.

Serving

Serve on a white platter with basmati and wild rice for a full, dramatic effect.

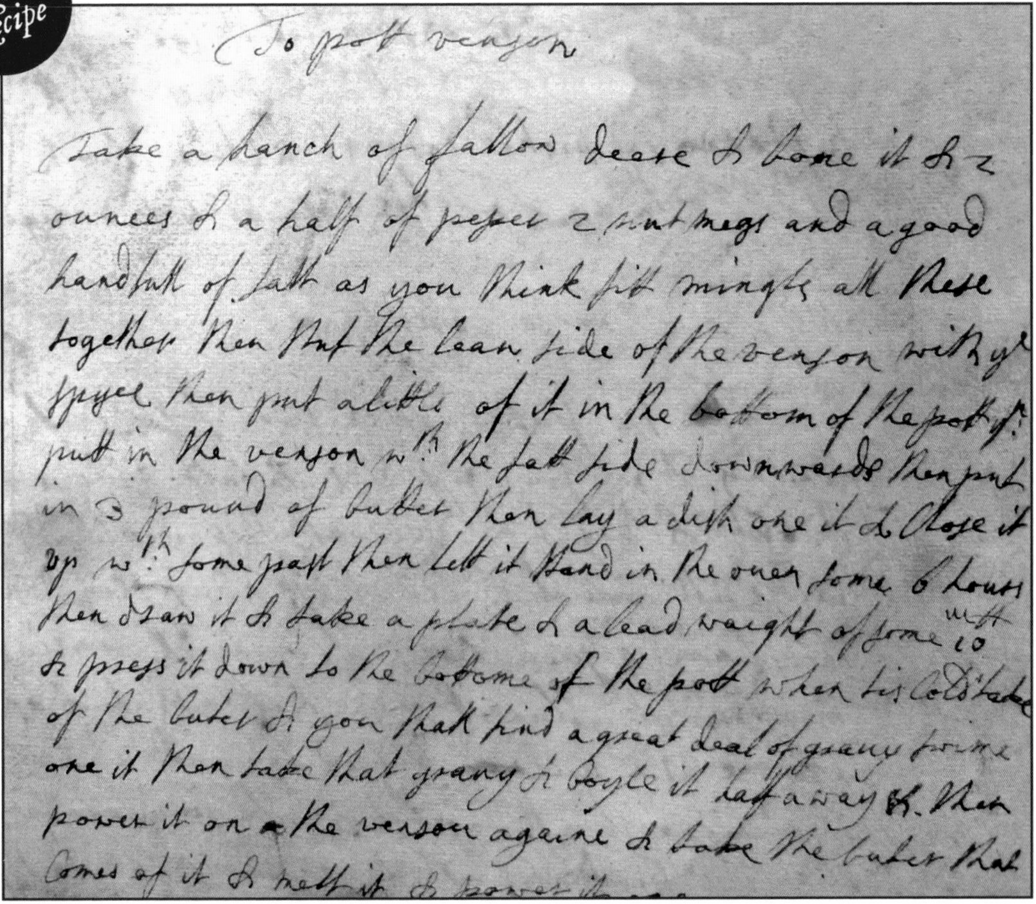

Recommended Wines

Australian Cabernet Sauvignon
Malbec
Southern Rhone GSM
Burgundy

Original Recipe

To pott venson

Take a hanch of fallow deere & bone it & 2 ounces & a half of peper 2 nutmegs and a good handfull of salt as you think fitt mingle all these together then rub the lean side of the venson with ye spyce then put alittle of it in the bottom of the pott & put in the venson wth the fatt side downwards then put in 3 pound of buter then lay a dish one it & close it up wth some past then lett it stand in the oven some 6 hours then draw it & take a plate & a lead waight of some 10 wt & press it down to the bottome of the pott when tis cold take of the buter & you shall find a great deal of gravy forme one it then take that gravy & boyle it half away & then power it on the venson againe & take the buter that comes of it & melt it & power it ...

'To Pott Venison', Ann Talbot, Lacock Abbey, 1745.

Venison Casserole with Allspice & Sherry

Also marinated for 24 hours, this has a deliciously different flavour. It is not so rich and dark as the Royal Venison Casserole, but the sherry gives it a sharper kick.

Serves 6-8

Ingredients

125g (½ cup) RAISINS
Zest and juice of 1 ORANGE
200ml (¾ cup) ORANGE JUICE
150ml (⅔ cup) DRY SHERRY
1kg (2¼lbs) VENISON
1tsp SALT
3 tbsp OIL
500g (3 cup) ONIONS, sliced
1tsp coarse ground BLACK PEPPER
½tsp crushed CORIANDER SEEDS
½tsp CINNAMON
½tsp GROUND MACE
Pinch of ALLSPICE
1½tbsp PLAIN (SOFT) FLOUR
750ml (3¼ cup) BEEF STOCK
2tbsp SHERRY VINEGAR

Method

1. Preheat the oven to 170°C (325°F).
2. Put the raisins, orange, orange juice and sherry in a bowl for a few hours or overnight.
3. Dice the venison and sprinkle with salt.
4. In a large pan, heat the oil and fry the venison until browned. Transfer to a casserole dish.
5. Put the sliced onions into the pan (adding a little more oil only if necessary) and fry until golden brown.
6. Add the pepper, spices, orange zest and flour to the pan and cook for 3 minutes. Pour in the stock and bring to the boil, adding the vinegar.
7. Pour the mixture over the meat in the casserole dish. Cover with the lid and cook in the oven for 1 hour.
8. Strain the raisins from the orange juice, add the juice to the casserole, and cook in the oven for another 1-1½ hours.
9. Add the raisins (keeping some back for the plate decoration), return the casserole to the oven, and heat through for about 5-10 minutes before serving.

Serving

Serve with mashed potatoes and
sprinkled with parsley and raisins
around the plate.

Recommended Wines

Chilean Merlot
Aglianco

Venison Steak

Venison was a royal favourite. Adding a marinade to venison transforms the taste. The steak does not have to be as thickly cut as for the beef fillet steaks or sirloin steaks.

Serves
6-8

Ingredients

Ask the butcher to cut tender
 LOIN STEAKS 2cm (¾in) thick
 (1 venison steak per person)
RED WINE, enough to cover the steaks
PORT, enough to cover the steaks
A sprinkle of MARJORAM
A little fresh, crushed GARLIC
3tbsp REDCURRANT JELLY
1tsp DRIED MUSTARD
1tsp GINGER, grated fresh
½ ORANGE, zest and juice
½ LEMON, zest and juice
BLACKBERRY JAM, to taste
RIPE SOFT FRUIT (like peaches, pears,
 or grapes), cut into small pieces
A handful of SHALLOTS,
 finely chopped

Method

TO MARINATE

1. Lay the venison in a china dish and cover with a mix of wine and port, proportionally ⅔ wine to ⅓ port.

2. Sprinkle with marjoram and freshly crushed garlic.

3. Cover with foil and leave, turning occasionally, for a maximum of 24 hours.

TO COOK

1. Make the sauce by warming together the redcurrant jelly, dried mustard, ginger, and the zest and juice of ½ orange and ½ lemon.

2. Add half of the marinade, boil for 2-3 minutes to reduce to ¾ volume (this concentrates the taste).

3. Taste and season.

4. Add blackberry jam to sweeten to taste.

5. Add more port to taste.

6. And some small bits of ripe soft fruit (like peaches, pears, or grapes) for texture.

7. Fry finely chopped shallots for more texture and add to the sauce.

8. Fry the venison for 2-4 minutes on each side - depending on thickness and how your guests like their meat.

Serving

Pour some sauce over the steaks, leaving the rest in a gravy boat and serve at once. Serve with small whole leeks, parsnips, and a pear in red wine, or with potatoes mashed with celeriac.

Recommended Wine

Chateauneuf-du-Pape
Rhone, Hermitage or Crozes
Shiraz

Crown Roast of Lamb & Roast Vegetables

This historic recipe needs careful cooking of its accompaniments - either stuffing, or colourful roast vegetables as given here - because they have to be cooked separately. The trick is not to overcook the vegetables.

Serves 6-8

Original Recipe

To roast a breast of mutton with oysters

Take a breast of mutton and a quart of oysters to a pint of them put the yolks of 2 Eggs beaten 2 or 3 spoonfulls of white wine sweet marjoram Time and winter savory shred small a little nutmeg grated an onion sliced and mix them well with half yr oysters then rip up the skin of yr mutton and fill it with yr oysters and put the liquor to it and seewer done the skin again and stuff the other part of the mutton with some of the bone set a dish under it when it is roasting bast it often with what drops from it and nothing else have ready boyld the other pint of oysters boyld only in their own liquor till they are almost dry dissolve or melt one in it and mix it with what drops from the mutton whilst it is roastning put in a peice and shake them well together and power it on yr mutton

'To roast a breast of mutton with oysters,' Ann Talbot, Lacock Abbey, 1745.

Ingredients

2 or 3 RACKS OF LAMB tied together to resemble a crown prepared by your local butcher (6-8 ribs each rack approximately 900g (2lb) each)

ROAST VEGETABLES

300g (11oz) PEARL ONIONS (red and yellow onions parboiled for 3 minutes and rinsed in cold water, tips removed, and peeled)

450g (1lb) small RED POTATOES, quartered

450g (1lb) small WHITE POTATOES, quartered

1 large TURNIP, peeled and cubed into 1¼cm (½in) pieces

2 large CARROTS, peeled and sliced into 1¼cm (½in) pieces

2tbsp PARSLEY (finely chopped)

COARSE SEA SALT and freshly ground BLACK PEPPER, to taste

MARINADE

(¾ of this mixture is for marinating the crown roast; the remaining ¼ is for sprinkling on the vegetables)

250ml (1 cup) OLIVE OIL

250ml (1 cup) WHITE WINE (Muscadet or similar)

4 CLOVES, crushed

1 ONION, finely sliced

1 CARROT, finely sliced

1 stick of CELERY, finely sliced

1tsp TARRAGON

2 ANCHOVIES, chopped

REDCURRANT JELLY AND WINE GRAVY

200ml (¾ cup) RED WINE

200ml (¾ cup) LAMB OR VEGETABLE STOCK

3tsp REDCURRANT JELLY

approx. 75g (¾ cup) PLAIN (SOFT) FLOUR

1tbsp FRESH MINT LEAVES, finely chopped

DECORATION

Enough DECORATIVE FRILLS for each bone (16-24) (sold in white paper, silver, or gold frills)

Recommended Wines

Faugeres
Rioja

Method

TO MARINATE THE LAMB

1. Pour ¼ of the blended marinade into the bottom of a deep round dish.
2. Sit the crown roast in the liquid (meat end down).
3. Baste, rubbing the marinade well into the centre and all sides of the lamb.
4. Place the dish with the crown roast carefully inside the large clear plastic bag.
5. Remove air from the bag and seal it.
6. Refrigerate for 24 hours.

NOTE: Any accompaniments to a crown roast (including roast vegetables) have to be cooked separately.

TO ROAST THE VEGETABLES

1. If you have two ovens, place the prepared vegetables in one or two baking trays (do not overcrowd).
2. Sprinkle sea salt and black pepper over the vegetables and toss them in the last ¼ of the marinade.
3. Roast for 30 minutes at 220°C (425°F), tossing every 10 minutes.

If you have one oven, you will need to roast the vegetables before the crown roast goes in, and keep them warm (without overcooking).

TO ROAST THE LAMB

1. Preheat the oven to 220°C (425°F).
2. Remove the dish from the bag and place the crown roast in a shallow roasting pan.
3. Use the marinade to re-baste the base, middle and sides of the lamb and let it stand at room temperature for ½ hour.
4. In order to cook the crown evenly, crumple a ball of tin foil to fill the centre of the crown. Protect the ends of the rib bone from burning in the oven by wrapping them loosely in individual tin foil 'hats'.
5. Roast in the oven for not more than 9 minutes per 450g (1lb) (approximately 35 minutes for 2 racks), basting every 10 minutes with melted butter or dripping. Be careful not to overcook.
6. Take the lamb out of the oven, removing the foil in the centre and the 'hats' around the bone tips.

TO MAKE THE GRAVY

1. Heat and thicken the redcurrant and wine with the flour and keep hot.

Serving

1. Carefully transfer the crown roast onto a serving platter, covering it completely with foil and tea towels.
2. Rest the joint for 10 minutes.
3. Just before serving, pile the potatoes and vegetables both inside the crown and around the edges, and sprinkle with parsley.
4. Drizzle a little gravy over the meat, and serve the rest in a gravy boat.
5. Allow 2-3 chops for each guest, with a little gravy poured over.

Pheasant, Partridge or Grouse with Cider & Caramelised Apple

Pheasant casserole was a favourite of Queen Victoria. She recorded a recipe for 'pheasant casserole with truffles, foie gras and Madeira wine' in her handwritten recipe book.

Serves
4

Original Recipe

To Stew Pidgeons —

To a dozen of Pidgeons grate two penny loaves, some bacon cut in bitts, then sweet margerum and parsley all shread small, Nutmeg, Mace, Pepper and Salt as you please, five Eggs beaten mix altogether into a forcedmeat, and put a little into each pidgeon, put them into a stew pan with their brest down wards, with as much water as will near cover them, when they are halfenough take another stew pan, and burn a quarter of a pound of butter and put them into it, and let them stew till they are enough, then by degrees put in the liquor they are stewed in so serve them, you may add mushrooms, oysters, or balls. —

Ingredients

2 PHEASANTS, OR 4 PARTRIDGES,
    or 4 GROUSE
RED WINE to cover
4½tbsp SUGAR
Big bunch FRESH THYME
80g (⅓ cup) BUTTER OR DRIPPING
10 whole SHALLOTS
1-2tbsp PLAIN (SOFT) FLOUR
SALT and PEPPER, to taste
600-800ml (2½ cup-3½ cup)
    CIDER (or Calvados)
10 COX APPLES (or other eating apple)

Any gamebirds can be used in the casserole, including pigeons. Lady Ivory, Lacock Abbey, wrote out this recipe 'To Stew Pigeons' in 1685.

Method

1. Remove the breast and leg meat from the birds.
2. Chop them into 2.5-4cm (1-1½in) pieces and marinate in red wine with 1 teaspoon of sugar and the fresh thyme (keeping a little thyme back for later) for 24 hours.
3. Preheat the oven to 170°C (325°F).
4. Heat the butter/dripping, fry the whole shallots until brown, and remove from pan into an ovenproof dish.
5. Quickly brown the game pieces, remove them from the pan and place with the shallots.
6. Add flour to the fat, stir and cook gently to thicken slightly, and add salt and pepper to taste.
7. Add the cider or Calvados, bring to the boil, and pour it over the game.
8. Make sure the liquid covers the birds. If necessary, top up with either strained marinade or more cider.
9. Put the rest of the thyme into the dish and cover.
10. Cook at 170°C (325°F) for 30 minutes, then leave to stand in a cool oven (120°C (250°F)) until ready (do not leave too long, or it will overcook).
11. Remove the thyme before serving.

NOTE: If using whole birds, cook in the oven at 170°C (325°F) for 45 minutes, then in a cool oven (120°C (250°F)) for 30 minutes.

To Serve with Apples

1. Skin, de-core, and cut the apples into quarters.
2. Put sugar in a saucepan, cover with water, and gently heat until the sugar is melted.
3. Boil the mixture until golden brown and pour it over the apples.
4. These can be left in a dish until you serve up the game.

Recommended Wines

Gigondas
Gran Reserva Rioja

'If partridge had the woodcock's thighs, 'Twould be noblest bird that flies; If woodcock had the partridge breast, 'Twould be the best bird ever drest.'

- Court Favourites

Pheasant Casserole with Dijon Mustard

Pheasants used to be farmyard animals like geese and ducks, and enclosed in fattening pens. The Dijon mustard in this dish brings out the rich flavour of the pheasant. This recipe is also good when cooking whole pheasants.

Serves
4

Ingredients

2 PHEASANTS
RED WINE, to cover
1 CARROT
1tsp SUGAR
1tbsp MUSTARD SEEDS
80g (⅓ cup) BUTTER OR DRIPPING
3 large ONIONS, finely chopped
1tbsp PLAIN (SOFT) FLOUR (plus
   a little more if required)
4tbsp DIJON MUSTARD
SALT and PEPPER, to taste
300–600ml (1¼ cup–2½ cup)
   SINGLE OR DOUBLE CREAM

Method

1. Either joint the pheasants or remove the meat from the breasts and legs.
2. If the meat is removed, chop pheasant into 2½-4cm (1-1½in) pieces and retain the pheasant bones to make a light stock by slowly simmering them in a saucepan with a chopped onion and carrot, and covered with water.
3. Marinate in red wine and sugar with mustard seeds for 24 hours.
4. Preheat the oven to 170°C (325°F).
5. Heat a large frying pan with butter or dripping and quickly fry the onions until soft.
6. Remove the onions and put them into an ovenproof dish.
7. Remove pheasants from the marinade, and dry on kitchen paper.
8. Reheat the butter/dripping and quickly brown the pheasants.
9. Remove them and put with the onions.
10. Strain the marinade.
11. Add a good tablespoon of flour to the dripping/butter and gently cook while stirring. Add the marinade and bring to the boil.
12. Add the Dijon mustard and salt and pepper to taste.
13. Bring back to the boil and add the cream.
14. Pour it over the pheasant to cover (add more stock if needed) and put the top on the ovenproof dish.
15. If the pheasants are in joints, cook for 45 minutes. If the meat is off the bone reduce the time to 30 minutes.

Serving

Rest the meat for 5 minutes before serving. Serve with mashed potatoes, large warm crisps, and broccoli.

Recommended Wine

Full Red Burgundy

Family
Meals

The Great Lamb Pie

Pies were great favourites at court down the ages. Every country house had a Great Pie. Lacock's, recorded by Lady Ivory in 1685, was made of lamb.

Serves
4-6

Ingredients

450g (1lb) LAMB LEG OR SHOULDER steak cut into small pieces
SALT and PEPPER, to taste
60ml (¼ cup) WHITE WINE
1tsp SUGAR
1 hard-boiled EGG
1 portion of HISTORIC PASTRY (see recipe and ingredients on page 96)
55g (½ cup) SWEET CHESTNUTS
60ml (¼ cup) DOUBLE (HEAVY) CREAM
1tsp GROUND GINGER
Beaten EGG to glaze

Method

1. Season the lamb with salt and pepper. Mix with white wine and sugar and leave to marinate for 24 hours.
2. Preheat the oven to 190°C (375°F).
3. Hard boil the egg, cool, peel and cut into quarters lengthwise.
4. Make the Historic Pastry, and reserve ⅓ for the lid.
5. Line a deep pie dish with foil, leaving enough over the side for lifting the cooked pie.
6. Roll out ⅔ of the pastry and line the dish on top of the foil.
7. Remove meat from marinade and retain the liquid.
8. Layer meat with chestnuts and hard-boiled eggs in the pie case.
9. Mix the cream with the marinade and ground ginger, and pour over filling.
10. Roll out the pie lid and place on top of the pie, crimping the edges to seal. Brush with beaten egg and make a hole in the top for the steam to escape.
11. Cook for about 1 hour.

'"One of my passions", Queen Elizabeth I said of the Royal Lamprey Pie. An over-indulgence killed off 2 Kings ... Henry I and his grandson King John. A 17th c Pie would surely cause unholy indigestion - often with ingredients like small birds, oysters, chestnuts, pickled berries, dates and eggs - all in the one pie.'

- Court Favourites

Original Recipe

How to Season a Lamb Pye
First take a hinder Quarter of Lamb and Season it with Nutmeg
Cinnamon and Salt and half a pound of Marrow amongst the
Meat, then lay it in the Pye with the meat some Slices of
Orringe and Lemmon Pill and Citteon Pill preserved, and then
Close it and when it is baked melt a Quarter of a pound of
Butter and a Pinte of White Wine and a Quarter of a pound
of white Powder Sugar and put these in the Pye. Shake it
and Serve it

'How to Season a Lamb Pye', Lady Ivory, Lacock Abbey, 1685.

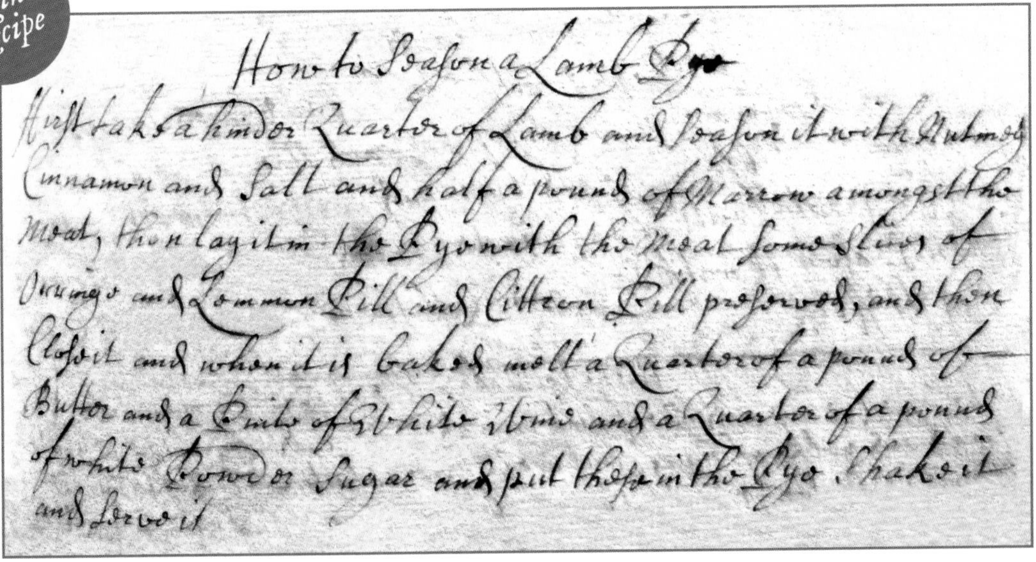

Lamb Pies

Lamb Pie was a great favourite for informal meals.

8 × 10cm pies

Ingredients

120ml (½ cup) RED WINE
1tbsp MIXED CURRANTS
    AND SULTANAS
½tsp CINNAMON
½tsp NUTMEG
1tsp SUGAR
225g (8oz) LAMB LEG OR SHOULDER
    STEAKS, cut into small pieces
55g (2oz) MARROW, cubed
1 portion of HISTORIC
    PASTRY (*see* p. 96)
Beaten EGG to glaze

Method

1. Preheat the oven to 190°C (375°F).
2. Mix the wine, currants, sultanas, spices and sugar to make the marinade. Pour it over the meat, stir and leave for 24-48 hours in the fridge.
3. Make the pastry. Reserve ⅓ for lids. Roll out the rest and cut circles about 10cm (4in) in diameter. Either hand raise or place in Yorkshire pudding tins.
4. Add the marrow to the meat mixture and place in the pastry.
5. Roll out the remainder of the pastry and cut lids to fit. Moisten the edges of the lids and lay them over the meat, crimping edges to seal.
6. Brush pies with beaten egg and cook for about 40 minutes.

Serving

Serve hot with potatoes and vegetables for supper, or cold as a snack.

Lemon & Ginger Lamb Pasties

Still properly called 'patties', these pasties are diminutive versions of big, hot pies originally served as hors d'oeurvres and as small entrées. They are best when eaten straight from the oven.

Serves
4

Ingredients

450g (1lbs) MINCED LAMB
150ml (⅔ cup) WHITE WINE
1tsp SUGAR
1 LEMON
1¼cm (½in) grated FRESH
    GINGER ROOT
1 portion of HISTORIC
    PASTRY (*see p.96*)
1 EGG, beaten
½tsp GROUND GINGER

Method

1. Preheat the oven to 190°C (375°F).
2. Mix the lamb mince with white wine, sugar, the zest and juice of a lemon and grated ginger root, and leave for 24-48 hours to marinate.
3. Make pastry and divide into four.
4. Roll out into circles about 23cm (9in) in diameter.
5. Divide lamb mixture between each circle and crimp up the edges to form upright pasties.
6. Mix the ground ginger into beaten egg and glaze the pasties.
7. Cook for 40 minutes.

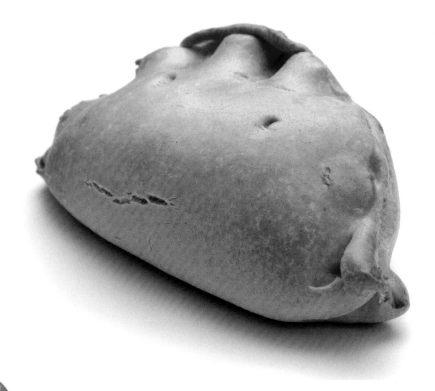

To Make Garlick Patties

Mince the Veal or any white meat that has been dress'd before
very small, & season it with a little pepper, & Salt, then Chop a
little Garlick very small and mixt it well in the meat then put
some Cream and Lett it Stew a Little while Together then cold put
it in puff paste and Bake them of a Lettish Brown

'To Make Garlick Patties', Lady Ivory, Lacock Abbey, 1685.

Historic Pastry

This Historic Pastry can be used on any pastry dish and is how pastry ought to taste. Try adding a sprinkle of herbs on the top of your pastry for additional flavour.

Makes
1 pie

Ingredients

175g (¾ cup) BUTTER
350g (3 cup) STRONG (BREAD) FLOUR
150ml (⅔ cup) HOT WATER

Method

1. Rub the butter into the flour until it resembles breadcrumbs.
2. Slowly add the hot water.
3. Mix well to form dough.
4. Use as required for your pie recipe.

Fish Pie

Fish pie has been a royal favourite for centuries. Henry I is reported to have tucked into a lamprey pie every Christmas.

Serves
4-6

Ingredients

250g (1⅓ fillets) HADDOCK OR COD
250g (½ fillet) SALMON
1 tin ANCHOVIES in oil (50g (2oz) size)
200g (¾ cup) PRAWNS
    (JUMBO SHRIMP)
2½cm (1in) FRESH GINGER, crushed
2-3 pieces WHOLE MACE
1 NUTMEG, broken into small pieces
50g (¼ cup) BUTTER
120ml (½ cup) FISH STOCK (or 120ml
    (½ cup) water and 1tsp fish granules)
A pinch of GRANULATED SUGAR
30g (¼ cup) PLAIN (SOFT) FLOUR

CRISPY MASHED POTATO
AND CHEESE TOPPING

500g (1lb 2oz) POTATOES
30g (2tbsp) BUTTER
A dash of CREAM
SALT and PEPPER, to taste
1 big handful of grated
    PARMESAN CHEESE

Method

TO MAKE THE TOPPING

1. Steam or boil the potatoes, then mash and add the butter and cream.
2. Keep warm until the pie is ready for the topping.

TO MAKE THE PIE

1. Preheat the oven to 200°C (400°F).
2. Chop the anchovies into small pieces, discarding the oil.
3. Put them into a saucepan with the fish stock and bring to a gentle boil.
4. Stir in a pinch of sugar and keep stirring to reduce the liquid slightly.
5. Add the haddock and salmon and lightly poach.
6. Remove the salmon and haddock, break them up gently, and place in a pie dish.
7. Remove some of the anchovies and add them to the dish.
8. Add the prawns.
9. Make a white sauce with melted butter, fish liquor (including the rest of the anchovies), ginger, mace, nutmeg, fish granules and flour.
10. Pour the sauce over the fish.
11. Cover the fish pie mixture with the mashed potato and sprinkle the cheese over the top.
12. Cook for approximately 20 minutes, until topping is brown and crisp.

'Prawns and shrimps from Morecombe Bay were dispatched weekly to the royal table of King George V.'

- Court Favourites

Curries

The following dishes use authentic curry mixtures from the archives of Thirlestane Castle, mixes formed before the influence of the British Raj changed the curry recipes of India.

The Thirlestane Castle Curries

With its rose-pink sandstone fairytale turrets and secret passages, Thirlestane is one of the oldest and finest castles in the land and it holds a unique and important place in Scottish history. It is home to the Lauderdales (family name Maitland) who are the most ancient noble family in Scotland. Family records include the manuscripts of Lt Col Frederick Henry Maitland, the 13th Earl of Lauderdale, who, as a young man, served in the Indian Army in the days of the Raj, just after the Indian Mutiny of 1857/8. He brought his Indian Army cook back to Scotland along with traditional Indian recipes.

All the ingredients can be bought in
an Indian supermarket or specialist
shop. It is worth buying bigger packets
of herbs and spices and keeping them
in store.

Original Recipe

> To make Curr
>
> Take a large Chicken and skin it cut it into
> Joynts 2 ounces of butter and put it in a stew pan
> and brown it well then put to it a bit of onyon
> cut in thin slices and take it out when its
> brown take two ounces of Jorden almond blanch
> and pounded to milk but Pastalioe nuts is
> better put them in when the Chicken is browne
> then season it with Turmerick and pounded
> pepper, mixe altogether to y' tast you may garnis
> y' sides of y' dish with boyld rice

'To Make Curry', Ann Talbot, Lacock Abbey, 1745.

Raj Curry Powder

This makes a creamy curry sauce that can be used on any light meat. You can adjust the heat to suit.

Serves 4-6 | V

Original Recipe

The Earl of Lauderdale, Thirlestane Castle Household Cookery Book, 1860.

Dry Ingredients

2tbsp CORIANDER
2tbsp TURMERIC
2tsp MILD CHILLI POWDER
(more or less to taste)
1tsp CLOVES, ground
1tsp MUSTARD SEEDS
1tsp CINNAMON
1tsp GARAM MASALA

Liquid Ingredients

1tbsp CORN OIL
2tsp GINGER PASTE
2tsp GARLIC PASTE
1tbsp TOMATO PURÉE
4tbsp YOGHURT

Method

1. Heat the corn oil gently in a wok.
2. Add all the dry ingredients and mix well.
3. Add in the ginger paste, garlic paste, tomato purée and yoghurt.
4. Place the mixture in a bowl with the meat to be used (approximately 700g (1½lb) meat, cubed).
5. Cover with cling film and place in the fridge for at least 1 hour to marinate before cooking.

A Milder Dry Curry & Herb Mix

This gives a little extra taste to poultry, red meat or fish, and it is wonderful sprinkled over sautéed potatoes.

Serves 4-6

Ingredients

100g (⅓ cup) SEA SALT
6-8 DRIED CHILLIES
6tsp CUMIN SEEDS
1tbsp CORIANDER SEEDS
1tsp BLACK PEPPERCORNS

Method

1. Shake all ingredients together, place on a baking tray and toast in the oven at 140°C (275°F) for 20 minutes.
2. Cool, then grind to make a fine powder.
3. Store in an airtight jar in the fridge.

A Slightly Stronger Curry Mix

A very simple blend, this is recommended to bring out the full flavour of roast chicken and roast pork.

Serves 4-6

Ingredients

1tbsp GARLIC POWDER
1tbsp CHILLI POWDER
2tbsp GROUND CUMIN
1tbsp GROUND SEA SALT
1tsp CASTER (TURBINADO) SUGAR

Method

1. Put all the ingredients into a bowl and mix them well together.
2. Store in an airtight jar in the fridge.
3. Fill a shaker with this and use to cover the meat all over.

Raj Curry Ingredients Found in these Recipes

Almonds	Blanched almonds are available whole, flaked, and ground, and impart a sumptuous richness to curries. A great delicacy in India, they are very expensive.
Basmati rice	If possible, try to use basmati rice for all your savoury rice dishes; the delicate flavour is unbeatable.
Bay leaves	The large dried leaves of the bay laurel tree are one of the oldest herbs in cookery.
Bengal gram	Bengal gram is used whole in lentil curries. The flour (besan) is used to prepare bhajias, and may be used to flavour and thicken curries.
Cardamom pods	Native to India, this is considered the most prized spice after saffron. The pods can be used whole or the husks can be removed to release the seeds. They have a slightly pungent but very aromatic taste. They come in green, white, and black; the green and white pods can be used for both sweet and savoury dishes, or to flavour rice. The black pods are used only for savoury dishes.
Chillies - dried red	These hot peppers are extremely fiery and should be used with caution. The heat can be toned down by removing the seeds before use. Dried chillies can be used whole or coarsely crushed.
Chillies - fresh	Green chillies have become indispensable to Indian cuisine. They are very rich in vitamins A and C.
Chilli powder	Also known as cayenne pepper, this fiery ground spice should be used with caution. The heat can vary from brand to brand, so adjust quantities to suit your tastebuds.
Cinnamon	One of the earliest known spices, cinnamon has an aromatic and sweet flavour. It is sold ready-ground and as sticks.
Cloves	Used to flavour many sweet and savoury dishes, they are usually added whole.
Coriander - fresh	This beautifully fragrant herb is used both in cooking and for sprinkling over dishes as an attractive garnish.
Coriander seeds	This aromatic spice has a pungent, slightly lemony flavour. The seeds are used widely, either coarsely ground or in powdered form, in meat, fish and poultry dishes. Ground coriander, a brownish powder, is an important constituent of any mixture of curry spices.
Cumin	'White' cumin seeds are oval, ridged and greenish-brown in colour. They have a strong aroma and flavour, and can be used whole or ground. Ready-ground cumin powder is widely available. Black cumin seeds are dark and aromatic, and are used to flavour curries and rice.

Garam masala	A mixture of freshly ground spices, typically black cumin seeds, peppercorns, cinnamon, cloves and black cardamom pods. Buy it ready prepared from an Indian store; they know how to get the best blends.
Garlic	This is a standard ingredient in most curries. It can be used pulped, crushed, or chopped. Whole cloves of garlic are sometimes added to dishes.
Ginger	One of the most popular spices in India, and also one of the oldest. Fresh ginger is an important ingredient in many curries, and is now widely available. Dried powdered ginger is a useful standby.
Mustard seeds - black	They are round in shape and sharp in flavour. Black mustard seeds are used for flavouring curries and pickles.
Tumeric	This bright yellow, bitter-tasting spice is sold ground. It is used mainly for colour rather than flavour.

Buttered Curried Chicken

Thirlestane Raj curry mixes have been used to create the following three modern dishes. You can play around with the strength of the curry.

Serves
4-6

Ingredients

300ml (1⅓ cup) PLAIN
    GREEK-STYLE YOGHURT
1½tsp CHILLI POWDER
¼tsp GROUND CLOVES
1tsp GARAM MASALA
1tsp PULPED GARLIC
1½tsp SALT
55g (¼ cup) GROUND ALMONDS
¼tsp CRUSHED BAY LEAVES
¼tsp GROUND CINNAMON
1tsp PULPED GINGER
400g (2⅓ cup) CHOPPED TOMATOES
900g (2lbs) CHICKEN, cubed
1tbsp CORN OIL
85g (⅓ cup) BUTTER
2 medium ONIONS, sliced
2tbsp FRESH CORIANDER, chopped
70ml (⅓ cup) SINGLE (LIGHT) CREAM

Method

1. Mix together the first 11 ingredients.
2. Add the chicken, mix again, and set aside.
3. Melt the butter in oil in a large frying pan and soften the onions for about 3 minutes.
4. Add the chicken mix and stir fry for 7-10 minutes.
5. Add half the coriander.
6. Pour over the cream, stir and bring to the boil.
7. Garnish with rest of the chopped coriander.
8. More chilli powder may be added, to taste.

Recommended Wines

Australian Chardonnay
Clare Valley Riesling
Pinot Gris

Butterd chickens

Take 3 or 4 chickens ye less the better, pick them
clean and put them in a pot, and a litle more then
half boyle them, then take them out and flea em
and cut em all into Joynts, then put em into a
sause pan and almost cover em, with ye same liquor
they were boyld in, then ~~~~ let em boyl til they are
tender, close coverd, then put in half a pound of
fresh butter broaken into bitts, then let it stew
often shakeing it, when ye liquor is thick shred
about a spoonfull of raw parsly, shaking it well togeth
put in some onion, or onion water, liting it sim
and keeping it shaking, if it is not sharp enough
put in a litle Juce of lemon and salt to y^r
tast, serve it up opon sipets

'Buttered Chickens', Ann Talbot, Lacock, 1745.

Curried Vegetable Side Dish

A proper Raj curry meal must have a vegetable accompaniment. This mixture of broccoli, cauliflower, beans and potatoes looks and tastes perfect.

Serves 4-6

V

Ingredients

225g (8oz) FRENCH BEANS

1 large CAULIFLOWER, cut into florets

1 head of BROCCOLI, cut into florets

3tbsp VEGETABLE OIL

2 ONIONS, sliced

4 GARLIC CLOVES, chopped

1 thumb-sized piece FRESH GINGER, peeled and chopped

1tsp MUSTARD SEEDS

½tsp CUMIN SEEDS

4 large TOMATOES, chopped

1tsp GROUND CORIANDER

1tsp GROUND CUMIN

1tsp GROUND TURMERIC

½tsp CHILLI POWDER

2 GREEN CHILLIES, deseeded and sliced

360ml (1½ cup) WATER, more if required

900g (2lbs) POTATOES, thickly sliced

Method

1. Parboil the beans with the cauliflower and broccoli florets for 2 minutes in a covered pan of lightly salted water. Strain gently and leave to cool.

2. Heat only 2 tablespoons of oil, and sauté the onions, garlic and ginger, stirring for about 6/7 minutes, until softened. Remove from pan and set aside.

3. Toast mustard and cumin seeds in a dry pan for about 30 seconds, stirring all the time.

4. Transfer the toasted seeds to the pan in which the onion mix was cooked and add the rest of the oil, the tomatoes, ground coriander, cumin, turmeric, and chilli powder, and cook for 5 minutes.

5. Add the onion mixture.

6. Season the potatoes well, and add with the chillies to the mix.

7. Add water and simmer for 10 minutes.

8. Add the cauliflower, beans and broccoli and cook for a further 8-10 minutes (until sauce has thickened and the vegetables are tender).

Curried Meatballs

These moist and tasty meatballs
are a perfect alternative
to curried chicken.

Serves
4-6

Ingredients

225g (8oz) MINCED BEEF
225g (8oz) MINCED PORK
1tbsp GARLIC PASTE
225g (1 cup) MASHED
    POTATO for binding
2tbsp CORIANDER
A little beaten EGG
SALT, to taste

SAUCE

2 small WHITE ONIONS,
    finely chopped
2tbsp CORIANDER
2tsp CHILLI POWDER
2tsp GARLIC PASTE
1tsp GROUND CLOVES
2tbsp TOMATO PURÉE
CHILLI, to taste
2tbsp TURMERIC
2tsp MUSTARD SEEDS
2tsp GINGER PASTE
1tsp CINNAMON
2tsp GARAM MASALA
4tbsp PLAIN YOGHURT

Method

1. Preheat the oven to 200°C (400°F).
2. Mix all the ingredients with a little beaten egg to bind, and cover in cling film.
3. Place in the freezer to set for 10-15 minutes only.
4. Shape into meatballs approximately 2½cm (1in) around and bake for 20 minutes.

TO MAKE THE SAUCE

1. Mix all the ingredients for the curry sauce and heat well without burning.
2. Pour the curry sauce over the meatballs.

Serving

Serve with pilau rice.

Recommended Wine

Lebanese Full Red

Desserts

Apple & Apricot Tansey

This is an adaptation of Ann Talbot's 1745 recipe for Tansey. It uses King Charles II's favourite fruit, apple and apricot.

Serves 6-8

V

Ingredients

4 large COOKING APPLES

3 DESSERT APPLES

6-8 FRESH APRICOTS

6tbsp UNSALTED BUTTER

6 large EGGS

4tbsp DOUBLE (HEAVY) CREAM

4tsp ROSEWATER

½tsp NUTMEG

4tbsp SUGAR

ICING (CONFECTIONER'S) SUGAR to decorate

LEMON , sliced, to decorate

Method

1. Preheat your oven grill to the hottest temperature.
2. Peel and core the apples, and cut them into thin slices.
3. Peel, stone and quarter the apricots.
4. Using a large frying pan, melt the butter over a medium heat, but do not let it get brown or burnt.
5. Add the apple slices and fry them for about 3 minutes, turning once, add the apricots, and cook for another 3 minutes until the fruit softens and begins browning at the edges.
6. While the fruit is frying, beat the eggs together with the cream, rosewater, nutmeg, and 2 tablespoons of sugar.
7. When the apples and apricots are nearly ready, pour the egg mixture evenly over the top.
8. Cook the tansey for about 3 minutes, until the bottom solidifies.
9. Remove the frying pan from the hob, and place it under the grill.

To Make a Tansey

Mrs Ellis

Take a quart of Cream, and 20 eggs without the whites, sweeten it with sugar to yr tast, grate in a little nutmeg, coolor it with the Juice of spinage, and green wheat, or green grass, wch must be strain-d, then thicken it in a sauce pan, the thickness of an hasty pudding, then fret it in yr pan, and bake it a little brown, squeeze lemon over it, and strew a little sugar, and cut some orange to garnish it,

'To Make a Tansey', Ann Talbot, Lacock Abbey, 1745.

10. Let it cook for no more than 2-3 minutes, until the egg mixture is cooked through.
11. Turn the Apple and Apricot Tansey upside-down onto a large flat plate, sprinkle it with the rest of the sugar and splash it with fresh lemon juice.

Serving

Serve with a sprinkling of icing sugar and decorate with sliced lemon.

The King's Favourite Pudding no. 1: Fresh Apricot & Apple Crumble

'The Kings Favrite Pudding. œppricocks & œpples Pele & coar ye œpples, pele & stoan ye œppricocks, & plac in pidsh Kova ye warta & paste. Cook ye pi hot & colurd.'

- For King Charles ll, Lady Ivory, Lacock Abbey, 1685.

Serves 6-8   V

Ingredients

FILLING

10 large FRESH APRICOTS, peeled and stoned
3 large (or 4 medium) COOKING APPLES
2 EATING APPLES
1-2tbsp SUGAR to taste

BEST NUTTY CRUMBLE*

200g (1⅔ cup) PLAIN (SOFT) WHOLEMEAL FLOUR
2tsp GROUND CINNAMON
½tsp FRESH NUTMEG, grated
75g (¾ cup) ROLLED OATS
200g (¾ cup) UNSALTED BUTTER, chilled and diced
75g (⅓ cup) LIGHT BROWN MUSCOVADO SUGAR

75g (⅓ cup) DEMERARA (RAW CANE) SUGAR (plus extra for sprinkling)
100g (⅔ cup) HAZELNUTS, broken into small whole pieces
Pinch of SALT

OR

SWEET PASTRY TOPPING

75g (⅓ cup) BUTTER
75g (⅓ cup) LARD
300g (2½ cup) PLAIN (SOFT) FLOUR
55g (½ cup) ICING (CONFECTIONER'S) SUGAR
25g (⅛ cup) GROUND ALMONDS
1 EGG
4tbsp ORANGE JUICE

Method

TO MAKE THE CRUMBLE

(Make at least 2 hours in advance)

1. Mix the flour, spices and oats in a bowl.
2. Rub in the butter to form a crumbly mixture.
3. Stir in the sugars, hazelnuts and a pinch of salt.
4. Cover the bowl, and leave in the fridge for as long as possible.

TO MAKE THE ALTERNATIVE PASTRY TOPPING

1. Rub the fat into the flour, icing sugar, almonds.
2. Separate the egg and reserve the white.
3. Combine the egg yolk and the orange juice.
4. Mix with the dry ingredients to create a soft dough (adding water if necessary), and roll out gently (do not make it too thin).
5. Keep until the pie is ready.

TO MAKE THE APRICOT JUICE

1. Peel the apricots and place the peel and 1½ dessertspoons of sugar in a small pan.
2. Cover with water and boil up slowly to reduce and concentrate the liquid.

TO MAKE THE PIE

1. Preheat the oven to 190°C (375°F).
2. Peel and core the apples and cut into eighths. Place them in a pie dish.
3. Cut the apricots into small pieces and add to the apples in the dish.
4. Strain and press the apricot juice through a wire sieve on to the fruit in the pie dish and mix well.
5. Add the rest of the sugar.
6. Scatter the crumble mixture over the fruit and sprinkle with a little extra demerara (raw cane) sugar OR make a sweet pastry lid for the pie using leftover bits of pastry to decorate, and brush the whole pie with the reserved egg white mixed with tiny cut-up pieces of apricot.
7. Cook at for approximately 45 minutes until golden.
8. For the crumble only: When done, put under a hot grill until it is brown and crunchy.

Serving

Serve hot with cream.

The King's Favourite Pudding no. 2: The Winter Alternative

This recipe is a winter alternative to the Apricot & Apple Crumble, to be used when fresh apricots are out of season.

 Serves 6-8   V

Ingredients

10-15 organic DRIED APRICOTS
  (without preserves)
820ml (3½ cup) HOT WATER
7 RUSSET APPLES
3 medium BRAMLEY APPLES
1 LEMON
CINNAMON
SUGAR, to taste
3 sheets of FILO PASTRY
55g (¼ cup) BUTTER

Method

1. Depending on their size, take 10-15 dried apricots, pour about 820ml (3½ cup) of hot water over them to cover well. Soak for 6 hours or overnight.

2. Drain the apricots, reserving the liquid and half an apricot for decoration. Purée the fruit.

3. Take 7 russets and 3 medium bramley apples. Peel and core them, and cut into halves.

4. Put the apples and the puréed apricots in a pan with the soaking liquid, a squeeze of lemon and a good pinch of cinnamon. If necessary, add more water to just cover the fruit.

5. Cook gently, removing the apple pieces as they become softened (don't let them become mushy).

6. Add sugar to taste, if required.

7. Put the fruit and liquid in a large pie dish and leave it to cool.

TO MAKE THE GATHERED AND
BUNCHED FILO PASTRY TOP

1. Preheat the oven to 220°C (425°F).
2. Cut the first sheet of pastry into quarters, keeping the other sheets completely covered with a damp cloth to prevent them drying out.
3. Take one quarter, pinch the pastry up in the centre and turn it over, so the corners are facing up and closer to each other.
4. Place the bunched filo piece on the top of the pie.
5. Repeat the process for the other three-quarters.
6. Repeat again for the other two whole sheets (in quarters), ensuring that the top of the pie is completely covered, with some just hanging over the sides.
7. Drizzle with melted butter.
8. Bake for about 30 minutes.

Serving

Serve cold.

Oranges with White Chocolate & Honeycomb Mousse

Hollowed-out oranges, with a delicious white chocolate mousse and honeycomb inside, inspired by Ann Talbot's 1745 recipe for 'Buttered Oranges'. This recipe can be made the day before.

 Serves 4

 V

Ingredients

4 medium ORANGES (1 per person)
3 EGG yolks
65g (⅓ cup) CASTER
    (TURBINADO) SUGAR
½tsp VANILLA ESSENCE
1½tbsp ORANGE LIQUEUR
200ml (¾ cup) DOUBLE
    (HEAVY) CREAM
75g (3oz) HONEYCOMB,
    in pieces and crushed
125g (4oz) WHITE CHOCOLATE

FOR SYRUP

Juice and pulp of the 4 ORANGES
100g (½ cup) CASTER
    (TURBINADO) SUGAR

Method

1. Cut off the tops of the oranges (leaving enough room to work inside the orange), and cut a very small slice across the bottom; enough to let the orange stand on its own.

2. Keep the lids for decoration and carefully take out all the juice, pulp and pips and put the empty oranges aside. Discard all the pips, but keep the juice and pulp to make a syrup later.

3. Whisk the egg yolks with the sugar until light and thick.

4. Add the vanilla and set aside.

5. Melt the white chocolate and only 1 tablespoon of the orange liqueur in a bowl set over a saucepan of gently simmering water.

6. Beat in the egg yolks and continue to whisk over the heat until the mixture is thick enough to leave ribbon trails when lifted on the spoon.

7. Whisk the cream until it starts to form peaks and carefully fold in the other ½ tablespoon of orange liqueur, then whisk the cream and liqueur again to full peaks.

8. Fold the cream and the honeycomb into the egg mixture.

9. Freeze the mousse in a glass bowl until the next day - alternatively, for at least 3-4 hours.

10. In a small heavy saucepan, make an orange syrup by dissolving 100g sugar in the juice and usable pulp of the 4 oranges. Stir well until it becomes thick and syrupy (depending on the thickness, add more sugar).

11. Leave to cool.

12. Remove from the freezer just before serving.

Serving

Fill the oranges with the cold mousse and arrange each orange on a pudding plate, surround with orange syrup. Decorate with candied oranges, lemons, and the lid of each orange, tilted to see the mousse inside.

Original Recipe

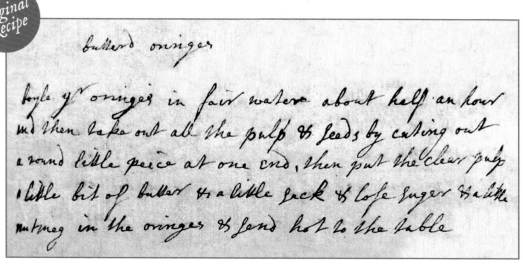

butterd orringes

boyle y^r orringes in fair waters about half an hour and then take out all the pulp & seeds by cutting out a round little peece at one end, then put the clear pulp a little bit of butter & a little sack & loafe suger & a little nutmeg in the orringes & send hot to the table

'Buttered Oranges', Ann Talbot, Lacock Abbey, 1745.

Royal Cherry Cheesecake

I know this makes a lot of cheesecake, but it will be so popular the next day! You can halve the mixture if you wish, but remember to use a smaller cake tin.

Serves 12		V

Ingredients

CHEESECAKE MIXTURE

250g (9oz) DIGESTIVE BISCUITS
125g (½ cup) BUTTER, melted
50g SUGAR (¼ cup) (first measure)
150g SUGAR (¾ cup) (second measure)
2 large EGGS
500g (2 cup) CREAM CHEESE,
    at room temperature
185ml (¾ cup) SOUR CREAM
1 ORANGE, zest grated and juiced

CHERRY PURÉE

200g (1 cup) stoned CHERRIES
85g (½ cup) SUGAR
(Plus a few drops of RED COLOURING
    if a brighter colour is desired)

When Queen Elizabeth I tried some cherries, presented to her by one of her Maids of Honour, she was so delighted with the taste it was said she never rested until 30 acres of the first cherry orchard in England was planted under her personal direction, in Kent.
Cherry pie was always a prominent dish at all her banquets from that time on.
Queen Henrietta Maria, Queen Anne, and King George III all claimed cherries to be the finest of all the fruits, and cherry pie the most delicious of all the sweets prepared in the Royal households.
Even Queen Victoria, aged 18, insisted upon cherries on the menu of her Coronation Banquet.

- Court Favourites

Method

1. Preheat the oven to 160°C (320°F).
2. Place the biscuits and the first measure of sugar into a food processor, and pulse to form crumbs.
3. Add the melted butter and combine. Then press the crumbs into the base of a 20cm (8in) spring-form cake tin, pressing down firmly.
4. Place the tin in the fridge and allow to cool completely.
5. Tip stoned cherries into a mixer with 85g (½ cup) sugar, blend until smooth, then tip into a small pan and bring to the boil.
6. Simmer for 5 minutes, stirring until it becomes a thick syrup.
7. Leave to cool (and add a few drops of red colouring if desired).
8. In a mixing bowl, beat together the cream cheese and the second measure of sugar until smooth.
9. Add the sour cream, eggs, orange zest and juice and beat well.
10. Pour the mixture into the prepared tin, then drop small spoonfuls of cherry purée evenly spaced over the top of the cheesecake mixture (using less than half the cherry mix).
11. With a broad knife, gently swirl the cherry colour through the cheesecake mix.
12. Cook for 30 minutes or until it is just set.
13. Allow the cheesecake to cool in the oven with door ajar for a further 30 minutes (do not let it go brown).
14. Take the cheesecake out and put it on the side to cool completely.
15. Refrigerate for several hours until perfectly set.

'For cheesecake - Take 3 pints of sweet & new milk and boyle it, & when it boyls, put therein 12 egg yolks, but only halfe of the whites, with a little salt.

Stir always over the fire till it comes to the curd.

Then strain the whey from it through a fine hair sieve.

When it is drained put it into a dish, stirring in a portion of fresh butter & a cup of thick sweet cream.

Season well with sack, rosewater, cleaned currants, cinnamon, sugar & all other spices pleasing to taste.

Half fill patty pans lined with puff paste, and bake.'

— *Court Favourites*

Serving

Serve with the remaining cherry purée on the side.

Cherry & White Chocolate Trifle

This uses Queen Elizabeth I's favourite fruit, cherries - with liqueur, brownies and white chocolate. Make sure the chocolate has enough egg white mixed in to be light.

 Serves 4

 V

Ingredients

500g (1lb 2oz) of CHERRIES in kirsch
3tsp SUGAR
400g (14oz) WHITE CHOCOLATE
400ml (1¾ cups) DOUBLE (HEAVY)
    CREAM, whipped
3 EGG whites, beaten
A few drops of RED COLOURING
8 CHOCOLATE MUFFINS, chopped

Method

TO MAKE THE CHERRIES AND KIRSCH

1. Drain the cherries and keep the kirsch.
2. Heat the kirsch with the sugar in a small pan and stir until the sugar has melted.
3. Put the cherries in a food processor until smooth.

TO MAKE THE WHITE CHOCOLATE MOUSSE

1. Break the white chocolate into small pieces.
2. Melt the chocolate in a bowl fitted over a saucepan of simmering water (care must be taken not to let the bowl touch the simmering water; white chocolate is more delicate than milk or dark - it will spoil if the bowl touches water).
3. Mix the melted white chocolate with the cream and fold in the beaten egg whites.
4. Mix half a teaspoon of whizzed cherries with enough colouring to make it a deeper red, then quickly swirl it through the mixture and set aside.

Assembly

1. Lay the chocolate muffin pieces at the bottom of a deep glass dish and pour over some of the kirsch (to soak into the muffin pieces). Leave to stand for at least 15 minutes.
2. Spread the cherries mixed with a little of the kirsch on the top.
3. Spoon on to the top the prepared white chocolate mousse (with its swirl of red).

Serving

Serve in one big, deep dish, or serve in individual coupe glasses, with several layers.

Raspberry & Ginger Cheesecake

A deliciously different cheesecake, with no cooking! This was inspired by Ann Talbot's 1745 recipe.

Serves
6-8

Ingredients

375g (13oz) GINGER BISCUITS
115g (½ cup) BUTTER, melted
3tsp POWDERED GELATINE
60ml (¼ cup) WATER
375g (1⅔ cup) CREAM CHEESE
1tsp VANILLA EXTRACT
220g (1 cup) CASTER
    (TURBINADO) SUGAR
250ml (1 cup) DOUBLE
    (HEAVY) CREAM
375g (3 cup) RASPBERRIES

Method

1. Place the biscuits in a food processor and process until the mixture resembles fine breadcrumbs.
2. Transfer to a bowl, add the melted butter and mix well.
3. Press into the base of a lightly greased 20x30cm (8x12in) tin lined with non-stick baking paper.
4. Refrigerate for 30 minutes or until firm.
5. Sprinkle the gelatine into the water and set aside for 5 minutes or until water is absorbed.
6. Beat the cream cheese, vanilla and sugar with an electric mixer for 4-5 minutes or until smooth.
7. Add the cream, and beat for 2-3 minutes or until thickened.
8. Gently fold in the gelatine and pour the mixture over the biscuit base.
9. Smooth with a spatula and top with raspberries, pointed ends up.
10. Refrigerate for 2 hours or until set.

'To Make Cheese Cakes', Ann Talbot, Lacock Abbey, 1745.

Serving

Serve in slices.

Meringues

The success of meringues depends on clean, dry cooking utensils. This recipe makes light brown meringues, gooey inside and scrumptious! They can be kept in a lined tin - but are best eaten fresh.

 Serves 4-6   V

Ingredients

3 medium EGGS, whites only
150g (⅔ cup) GOLDEN CASTER (TURBINADO) SUGAR
420ml (1⅔ cup) DOUBLE (HEAVY) CREAM

They were called 'Tentations' in the 1600s, a favourite of Queen Henrietta Maria (wife of King Charles I). The tradition at Coronation and Royal Banquets was for the chief Lady-in-Waiting to present them to the King and Queen; to prove the food was not poisoned, she kissed the cloth they lay on. Sometimes Meringues are still called 'Kisses'.

- Court Favourites

Method

1. Put a mixing bowl into the fridge for 30 minutes to get cold. Take out and wipe very dry.
2. Preheat the oven to 180°C (350°F).
3. Cut a sheet of baking parchment and put onto a baking tray.
4. Check your utensils are extra clean.
5. Make sure the sugar is ready beside your mixer.
6. Whisk the egg whites at high speed into stiff peaks.
7. Keeping the mixer running, add the sugar, 1 teaspoon at a time.
8. Continue whisking until it is stiff and shining.
9. Carefully spoon all of the mixture onto the parchment cooking paper in approximately 2½-4cm (1-1½in) rounds with peaks. (6 people will need 12 small rounds, 4 will need 8 larger ones.)
10. Place in the middle of the oven for 50 minutes, until they are light brown.
11. Do not open the oven door while they are cooking.
12. Meanwhile, wash the bowl and mixer blades, and dry carefully again.
13. Whisk the cream (it will be ready quite quickly) and let it stand until the meringues are ready.
14. When the meringues are out of the oven, remove them from the parchment and let them cool on the side for at least 30 minutes. Do not cover.

Serving

Before serving, sandwich the cream between two meringues. Alternatively, serve with fresh apricot whipped cream. (Ripe fresh apricots, peeled, stoned and mashed roughly with sugar. Add this mixture to the whipped cream just before it is sandwiched between the meringues.)

Syllabub

Also known as 'Sulebubbles' or 'Sillybubbles', Lady Ivory wrote out a recipe for 'Sillibub' in 1685. Queen Victoria also recorded a version in her handwritten cookbook that was made when she was a girl.

 Serves 6

 V

Ingredients

500ml (2 cup) DOUBLE
(HEAVY) CREAM
SUGAR, to taste
580ml (2½ cup) SWEET WHITE WINE
Other flavours: MADEIRA, MARSALA,
PORT, OR LEMON PEEL

Method

1. Sweeten the cream with sugar to taste.
2. Beat 580ml (2½ cup) of sweet white wine into the cream using a bunch of rosemary stalks.
3. As the froth rises, take it off, and put it into your individual syllabub cups.

Original Recipe

To make a syllibub
Take a pinte of the seconde skimming of your creame, and sweeten it with suger, then take almost a pinte of whitewine, and heate them all together with a birch rodd, or a Rosemary sticke, and as the froth riseth take it off, and put it into the Sillibub cupp.

'To Make a Sillibub', Lady Ivory, Lacock Abbey, 1685.

SULLIBUB UNDER THE COW

Pour a bottle of ale, cider,
or red or white wine into a china bowl.
Sweeten with sugar. Grate in nutmeg to taste.
Hold the bowl under a cow
and milk into the bowl
until a fine froth covers the top.
Strew a handful of cleaned,
washed currants over the froth.

- Court Favourites

Sweet Wine Ice Cream no. I

This recipe shows it is possible to create a new dish from the same ingredients as the Syllabub recipe by just adjusting the proportions.

 Serves 4-6

 V

Ingredients

150ml (⅔ cup) SWEET WHITE WINE (such as Orange Muscat)

3tbsp (rounded) CASTER (TURBINADO) SUGAR

300ml (1⅓ cup) carton DOUBLE (HEAVY) CREAM

Method

1. Tip the white wine and sugar into a bowl and whisk together.
2. Gradually whisk in the cream until it starts to thicken and just holds its shape.
3. Pour into a rigid container and freeze until firm - about 3-4 hours.
4. Take out of freezer about half an hour before use.

Serving

Serve in scoops with seasonal fruits splashed with a little more sweet white wine.

Sweet Wine Ice Cream no. 2

This modern recipe shows
how little ice cream recipes
have changed over the years.

 Serves 4-6

 V

Ingredients

150ml (⅔ cup) SWEET WHITE WINE,
 such as Orange Muscat

200ml (¾ cup) DOUBLE
 (HEAVY) CREAM

3 EGG yolks mixed with 2tbsp CASTER
 (TURBINADO) SUGAR

30g (⅛ cup) (more if necessary)
 CASTER (TURBINADO) SUGAR

Method

1. Tip the wine into a small strong saucepan
 with a cooking thermometer in.

2. Boil and reduce to 30g (slightly more than half
 the volume). This intensifies the flavour.

3. Remove the wine from the saucepan
 and cool in a fridge.

4. Using the same saucepan, add the cream and whisk in
 the egg yolks, extra sugar, and finally the cooled wine.

5. Keep stirring and slowly warm the mixture to
 70°C (160°F), so it coats the back of a spoon.

6. Chill in the fridge and then freeze.

Serving

This can be served almost straight from the freezer.
You only need to take it out of the freezer when you
serve up the main course. Serve with fan wafers.

Best Restaurant-Standard Ice Cream

The eggs and the cooking makes this ice cream rich, soft, pasteurised and long-lasting.

Serves 6-8   V

Ingredients

750ml (3¼ cup) FULL-FAT MILK
800ml (3½ cup) DOUBLE
    (HEAVY) CREAM
175g (¾ cup) CASTER
    (TURBINADO) SUGAR
6 EGG yolks

For other flavours, replace the
750ml (3¼ cup) milk with puréed
blackcurrants or other fruit
and more sugar (to taste).

Method

1. Poor the milk and cream into a saucepan and whisk in the egg yolks and sugar.
2. Stirring continuously, slowly warm the mixture to 70°C (160°F), so it coats the back of a spoon.
3. Chill in the fridge and then freeze.

Mary Queen of Scots Mousse

This recipe dates from 1569 and has been updated to make it suitable for today. This can be used as a dessert in its own right, but Mary Queen of Scots liked it layered with vanilla ice cream.

Serves
3-4

Ingredients

3 EGG yolks
A small pinch SALT
½tbsp UNFLAVOURED GELATINE
¾tbsp WATER
125ml (½ cup plus 1tbsp) MAPLE SYRUP
2 whole STAR ANISE
(250ml) (1 cup) DOUBLE
 (HEAVY) CREAM

Original Recipe

To Make Snow Cream

Ann Talbot would not have had the facilities to make ice cream but she did have this recipe for 'Snow Cream', Lacock Abbey, 1745.

Method

1. Whisk together the egg yolks and salt in a mixer on medium speed.

2. In a small bowl, sprinkle the gelatine over the water in a cup and let this stand.

3. With a thermometer and a heavy saucepan, mix the maple syrup with the star anise over a medium heat and boil until the syrup is 115°C (240°F) (it will boil, foam, and reduce at that temperature).

4. Remove the star anise and discard.

5. With the mixer on medium-high speed, slowly pour the hot maple syrup down the side of the bowl into the yolks.

6. Using a rubber spatula, scrape the gelatine into the empty pan in which you cooked the maple syrup and let it melt to a syrupy liquid.

7. Pour the gelatine into the egg yolk mixture, and whisk at medium-high speed until it triples in volume and cools to room temperature.

8. Whip the cream to soft peaks.

9. Fold it into the mousse with a flat spatula, using big long strokes, scraping the bottom and sides and ensuring that all of the cream is combined.

Serving

Seve a portion of mousse in between two slices of Best Restaurant-Standard Ice Cream (p. 140).

Best Possett Brûlée

This is one of the oldest puddings in culinary history. It looks like clotted cream on top and has a cheesy texture on the bottom. Lady Ivory recorded this recipe in 1685.

Serves 4-6

V

Ingredients

300ml (1¼ cup) DOUBLE
(HEAVY) CREAM
A blade of MACE
¼ NUTMEG
4 EGGS (using only 2 of the whites)
150ml (⅔ cup) SWEET SHERRY
55g (¼ cup) CASTER (TURBINADO)
SUGAR plus extra on
top for the brûlée

Method

1. Preheat the oven to 130°C (260°F).
2. Boil the cream in a saucepan with the mace and nutmeg and leave to one side.
3. Beat 4 egg yolks and 2 egg whites with sweet sherry in a bowl.
4. Add the sugar, then strain the mixture into a second clean bowl.
5. Set the bowl on a pan of simmering water and stir constantly until it thickens.
6. Pour the cream through a sieve into a jug, and then into ramekins.
7. Put the ramekins in a bain marie, cover with a lid or silver foil, and put in the oven for 25 minutes.
8. When cold, cover with cling film and chill in the fridge.
9. Just before serving, sprinkle caster sugar on top of the possett (about 0.5cm (⅛in) thick), and blow-torch or grill until it melts and takes colour.

Variations

1. For a surprise at the bottom, add small pieces of praline sprinkled in the base.
2. The above recipe also makes an extra delicious topping for a trifle.

The best posset – 5

Take a quart of good Creme. and boyle it with a blade of mace &
nutmeg Cut in quarters then take 14 Eggs leue out hafe the whites, beat them we
with a pint of sack. put hafe a pound of fine suger to it, and straine it all
through a haire Ciue in to your bason, then let it on a Chafeing dish of Coles,
keepe it stirring Constantly tell it begins to thicken, then poure the Creme pretty
on it. hold it a good haith when you poure it that it may froth, then mieing
couer it, with a pye plate. and keepe it upon ye Coles tell it be Come at the
bottom like a Cheese, and so serue it up without stirring it, ──

'The best posset', Lady Ivory, Lacock Abbey, 1685.

Sack Possett

An alternative possett with
both sherry and ale.

 Serves 4

 V

Ingredients

1 EGG yolk and 3 whites
300ml (1¼ cup) DOUBLE
(HEAVY) CREAM
CINNAMON STICK
WHOLE NUTMEG
2 flakes MACE
SUGAR, to taste
60ml (¼ cup) CREAM SHERRY
60ml (¼ cup) PALE ALE

Method

1. Whisk the egg whites until
frothy like meringue, and leave aside.
2. Bring cream, cinnamon, nutmeg and mace slowly
to the boil and let it steep for as long as possible.
3. Remove the spices and reheat.
4. Add the yolk while stirring (so it will
not curdle) and sweeten to taste.
5. Bring sherry and ale to the boil, take it off the heat
and add the whites, stirring until fully mixed in.
6. Add the cream, taste and sweeten again if necessary.
7. Pour into a dish, and put in the fridge to cool.

Serving

Serve each portion with a fan wafer.

Alternative

This sack possett is also great served hot, with a light layer of small crumbled digestives sprinkled over the top.

To Make a possett

Beat the Whits of a dozen new laid eggs w.th a birch rod & boyle a quart of Cream w.th a stick of Cinomin a nutmeg & a blade of maced — Thicken it with 5 yolks & sweeten it then take a pint of Sack & ale & set it in a bason one inbers & make it boyling hot then take the whits & put suger to them & power it into the Sack & ale & the Cream one the tyee boyling hot & stir it all together very gently

'To Make a possett', Ann Talbot, Lacock Abbey, 1745.

Old Irish
Flummery

The possetts from Lacock remind
me of family parties at Castletown,
my childhood home. This Flummery
recipe calls for oatmeal on
the top, but an alternative is a
light sugary brûlée crust.

Serves
4

V

Ingredients

1tbsp of OATMEAL
300ml (1⅓ cup) DOUBLE
  (HEAVY) CREAM
1tbsp HONEY (runny)
4tbsp of DRAMBUIE
Juice of ½ LEMON

Method

1. Heat the oatmeal while stirring in a
   heavy-based pan until brown.
2. Set aside to cool.
3. Beat the cream until smooth, but not stiff.
4. Melt the honey over a gentle heat until
   it runs easily (do not let it boil).
5. Fold the honey into the beaten cream, and
   finally stir in the Drambuie and lemon juice.

Serving

Serve the mixture in individual glasses or
dishes. Sprinkle oatmeal on top (or sprinkle
white sugar on the top, about 0.5cm (⅛in) thick
and either flambé or put under a hot grill to
brown and form a delicious hard crust).

Cheese Board Selection

These cheeses have been specially selected to represent the whole spectrum of flavours, from the aged to the familiar, from creamy to red, from smoked or blue to sharper, matured textures. If you want to complete your dinner-party experience, serve a dark, luxurious clear Miel honey as an accompaniment to any cheese.

Cheese Etiquette

If you are offering a large cheese board, arrange the mildest on the left-hand side (so they are eaten first), with the strongest on the right. You can also serve chutney, grapes, celery, apples, walnuts, and figs on and alongside the cheese board.

Buying Guide

Allow 80g of cheese per person.

To Keep Cheese

I prefer to buy it fresh, and house it temporarily under a cheese cloche at room temperature. Otherwise, wrap tightly in cling film or waxed paper and store in the salad drawer of the fridge, taking out 1 hour before serving.

A Selection of Cheese Biscuits

Bath Olivers
Cream crackers
Table water crackers
Wholemeal digestives
Cracked black pepper oatcakes

VINTAGE RED FOX	A vibrant mature Red Leicester. An intense and complex blend of sweet and savoury flavours.
OLD WINCHESTER (from Salisbury)	A Gouda-style cheese. The curd is washed to make it milky-white and sweeter.
ST ENDELLION	Made with Cornish double cream. A full-bodied soft cheese, deliciously tangy and rich. Suitable for the cheese board and for grilling.
CROPWELL BISHOP CLASSIC AGED BLUE STILTON	Supreme Champion International Cheese. Perfect with puddings, wine, port, dry sherry, claret, walnuts, honey, and pears.
CERNEY GOATS' MEDIUM-FAT SOFT GOATS' CHEESE	Fresh, creamy and mild flavour. A 'British Cheese Award' winner.
QUICKES TRADITIONAL VINTAGE CHEDDAR	A full-bodied taste, matured over 2 years. Best British Cheddar Award winner.
ST ALBRAY	A French soft cheese, like a rich mellow Camembert and shaped like the petals of a flower. The reddish-white rind is eaten as well. An interesting shape on a cheese board.
ST AGUR	French blue double-cream cheese. Mild and creamy. Also melts well in sauces.
APPENZELLER	Classic mild hard Swiss cheese, made for at least 700 years. Straw-coloured, with tiny holes and a golden rind. Wrapped in a silver label.
AGED OSSAU-IRATY	Traditional, unpasteurised semi-soft sheep's milk cheese from the French Pyrenees, with a sweet, buttery, fruity, and faintly nutty flavour. World Champion Awards winner.
BRIE DE MEAUX	The richest and creamiest unpasteurised French brie. Historically named 'The King of Cheeses'.
CAMEMBERT LE CHATELAIN	A French cheese from Normandy. It has been only gently pasteurised, so retains its original ripe, rich and creamy flavours.
VACHERIN DU HAUT-DOUBS-BADOZ	A seasonal delight. A soft young unpasteurised cheese, with a runny centre. Considered one of the best artisan cheeses from France.

Cakes

These cakes are little changed from those in
Tudor and Stuart times, just with updated
ingredients. They did use many more soft fruits
in their cakes, like the Raspberry Cakes here.
The oldest cakes here are the Meringue Kisses
(which could be hollowed out and filled with cream),
the 'Maids of Honour' Cakes,
and the Duke of York's Cake.

The Duke of York's Cake

This was a favourite of
King Charles II's brother, James, Duke
of York, the future King James II.
The recipe has been adapted to
make one large teacake, for slicing
and spreading with butter.

| Serves 10 | | V |

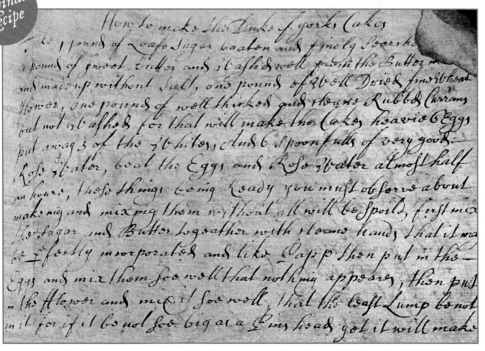

'How to make the Duke of Yorks Cakes', Lady Ivory, Lacock Abbey, 1685.

Ingredients

3 EGGS

2tbsp ROSE WATER EXTRACT

110g (½ cup) SUGAR

110g (½ cup) BUTTER

225g (2 cup) SELF-RAISING FLOUR

55g (¼ cup) CURRANTS

55g (¼ cup) SULTANAS

75g (⅓ cup) GLACÉ GINGER

Method

1. Preheat the oven to 180°C (350°F).
2. Beat the eggs and rose water together and set aside.
3. Mix the sugar and butter together.
4. Add the eggs and rose water and mix well.
5. Add the flour and mix again.
6. Add currants, sultanas and glacé ginger, and mix.
7. Pour the mixture into a 900g (2lb) lined loaf tin (or two 450g (1lb) tins) and bake for about 30 minutes.
8. Remove from the oven and cool on a cooling rack.

Serving

Serve this sliced as a buttered tea bread, decorated with sugar crystal.

Queen Victoria's journal re Queen Anne, 1708.

A Good Drink of Tea

Make a quart of very
excellent brewed tea,
Pour it out and set
it over the fire,
& beat therein the
yolks of 4 eggs & a
pint of white wine,
& grated nutmeg,
and sugar to taste.
Stirr over the fire
till very hot.
Drink it in china dishes.

- Court Favourites

Rich Fruit Cake

This was inspired by a recipe for 'The Royal Wedding Cake' recorded by Queen Victoria. The recipe was probably originally created for the wedding of King George III in 1761.

 Serves 10

 V

Ingredients

1.125kg (5½ cup) MIXED DRIED FRUIT
110g (½ cup) GLAZED CHERRIES
140ml (⅔ cup) SHERRY
225g (1 cup) BUTTER
225g (1¼ cup) DARK BROWN SUGAR
6 EGGS, beaten
300g (2½ cup) PLAIN (SOFT) FLOUR
½tsp BAKING POWDER
55g (⅔ cup) GROUND ALMOND
2tsp MIXED SPICES
1½tbsp BRANDY

'For Royal Wedding Cake - First work the butter in a large white pan with a wooden spoon until it presents the appearance of a creamy substance. Next add by degrees, the sugar, flour, salt and eggs, still continuing to work the batter the whole of the time. Then add the remainder of the ingredients and as soon as all is thoroughly incorporated, let the preparation be poured into a proper-sized tin hoop, previously lined with a double band of buttered paper, and ready placed upon a stout baking sheet, the bottom of which must also be lined with double sheet of paper. Bake in a moderate heat and be careful not to increase the heat of the oven while baking. A cake of this weight will require about four hours' baking.'

- Court Favourites

Method

1. Soak the mixed dried fruit and glazed cherries (cut in halves) in the sherry for 24 hours.
2. Preheat the oven to 140°C (275°F).
3. Cream together the butter and dark brown sugar and mix all the ingredients together.
4. Line a cake tin (20cms (8in) round) and grease it well.
5. Add the mixture.
6. Before putting the cake in the oven, put 580ml (2½ cup) of boiling water in a container to help keep it flat.
7. Cook at 140°C (275°F) for 45 minutes, then reduce the heat to 120°C (250°F) and cook for about 3-4 hours.
8. Put brandy in the cake once it is cool, and leave the tin overnight, upside down on a wire rack.
9. Wrap the cake in baking paper, then foil, and store for at least nine weeks. It is well worth the wait!

'Maids of Honour' Cakes

Tudor and Stuart cakes from the royal palaces are still popular today. 'Maids of Honour' Cakes, for example, are still made in Richmond, Surrey, the location of Richmond Palace. The following recipe was printed in *Court Favourites*.

Serves 4-6 | V

Ingredients

55g (¼ cup) SUGAR
55g (¼ cup) BUTTER
25g (¼ cup) DESICCATED COCONUT
1 beaten EGG
1 LEMON, grated rind,
    and strained juice
1tbsp COOKED SAGO (TAPIOCA)
175g (6oz) PUFF PASTRY

Method

1. Preheat the oven to 220°C (425°F).
2. Beat sugar and butter to a cream.
3. Stir in desiccated coconut, a beaten egg, the grated rind and strained juice of the lemon and a tablespoon of cooked sago.
4. Half fill a patty pan tin lined with puff pastry.
5. Bake in a hot oven for about 15 minutes.

Violet Cakes

Lacock made cakes from all sorts of edible flowers and fruit. These cakes can be quite the talking point at tea parties and were inspired by Lady Ivory's 1685 recipe.

Serves 6–8

V

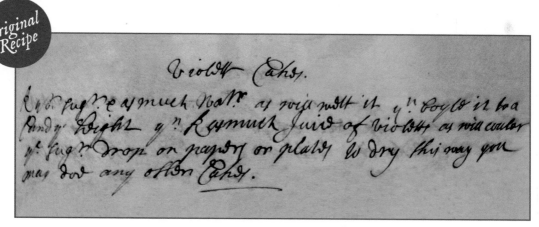

'Violet Cakes', Lady Ivory, Lacock Abbey, 1685.

Ingredients

175g (1 cup) BUTTER
175g (1 cup) CASTER
    (TURBINADO) SUGAR
175g (1½ cup) SELF-RAISING FLOUR
3 EGGS, beaten
1tbsp of VIOLET SUGAR
    (VIOLET EXTRACT and
    SUGAR to taste)
Small amount of
    READY-TO-ROLL SUGAR
    PASTE (FONDANT) with
    VIOLET EXTRACT added

FILLING

110g (½ cup) BUTTER
225g (2¼ cup) ICING
    (CONFECTIONER'S) SUGAR
VIOLET EXTRACT, to taste

Method

1. Preheat the oven to 180°C (350°F).
2. Mix butter and caster sugar well.
3. Add self-raising flour and eggs, mixing well.
4. Add violet sugar and mix again.
5. Pour the mixture into muffin cases inside muffin tins, filling to ¼ full.
6. Cook for about 12 minutes.
7. Meanwhile, cream the butter and icing sugar, adding violet extract (add a little water if it is too thick).
8. When the cakes are cool, cut out a small amount of the middle and fill first with violet sugar, followed with violet butter cream.
9. Cover the top of the muffins with cut-out round sugar paste (fondant), and top each one with fresh violet (or cut-out sugar paste violets) for decoration.

Raspberry Cakes

This is based on
Ann Talbot's 1745 recipe
for 'Rasberry Cakes'.

Serves 6-8

V

Ingredients

175g (1 cup) BUTTER
175g (1 cup) CASTER
 (TURBINADO) SUGAR
175g (1½ cup) SELF-RAISING FLOUR
3 EGGS, beaten well
1½tbsp FREEZE-DRIED RASPBERRIES

FILLING

A punnet (pint) of RASPBERRIES
1tbsp HONEY
55g (⅓ cup) SOFT CHEESE
A little SOFT ICING (for top)

Method

1. Preheat the oven to 180°C (350°F).
2. Mix the butter and sugar, then add the flour
   and eggs a little at a time, mixing well.
3. Add ¼ of the freeze-dried raspberries and mix again.
4. Put the mixture into muffin cases inside muffin tins.
5. Fill the cases ¾ full and cook for
   about 12 minutes or until firm.
6. Meanwhile, put most of the fresh raspberries,
   honey and soft cheese into a pan.
7. Bring the pan to the boil, turn heat to low,
   and mash the mixture until it begins to thicken.
8. Remove it from the heat and leave to cool.
9. When the cakes are cooked and cool, remove the
   centre and add some dried raspberries, followed
   by the raspberry, honey and soft cheese mash.
10. Cover the tops with raspberry icing (soft icing
    with a little raspberry to give colour).
11. Add a fresh raspberry for decoration.

To make Rasberry Cakes

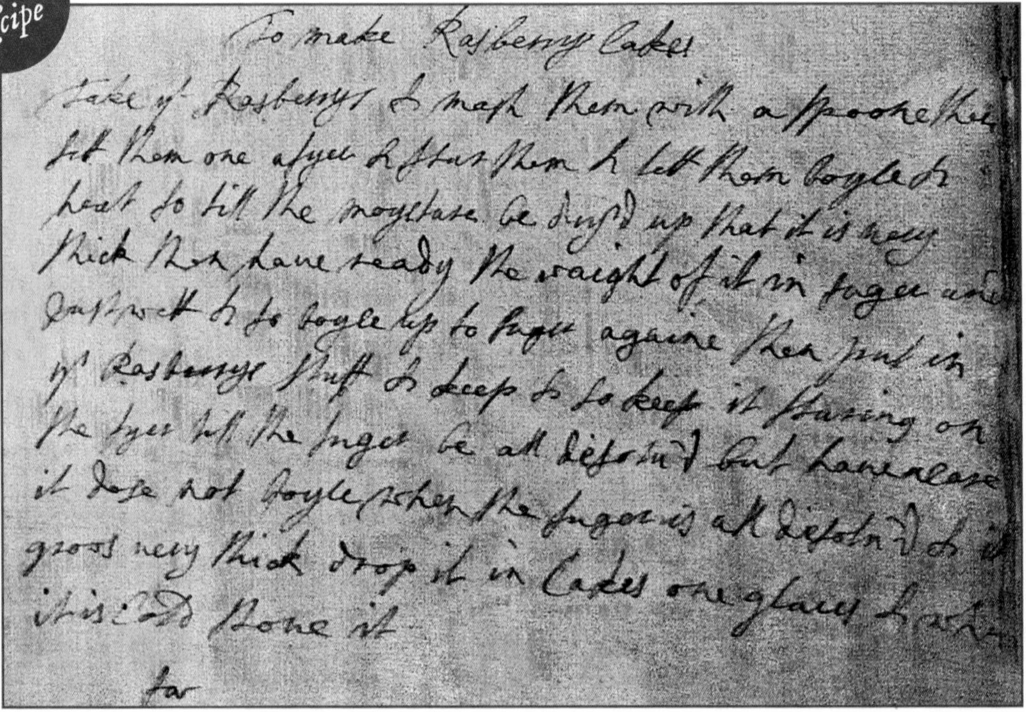

take y Rasberys & mash them with a spoone then
set them one a fyer & stur them & let them boyle &
beat so till the moystase be dryd up that it is very
thick then have ready the waight of it in suger and
put well & to boyle up to suger againe then put in
y Rasberys stuff & keep & so keep it stering on
the fyer till the suger be all dissolved but have a care
it dose not boyle when the suger is all dissolved & it
grows very thick drop it in cakes one glass & when
it is cold stove it

        for

'To make Rasberry Cakes', Ann Talbot, Lacock Abbey, 1745.

Orange Meringue Kisses

These small meringues were often served at royal teatime, hollowed out and filled with cream. For this recipe, you will need a jam-making thermometer.

Serves 6 — V

Ingredients

150g (¾ cup) SUGAR
4 EGG whites
2tsp ORANGE EXTRACT
10 drops YELLOW FOOD COLOURING
2 drops RED FOOD COLOURING
175g (6oz) WHITE CHOCOLATE, melted

Method

1. Preheat the oven to 200°C (400°F).
2. Whisk the sugar and egg whites together in a bowl set over a pan of simmering water, and stir until the mixture reaches 140°C (275°F).
3. Remove the bowl from the pan and, using a hand mixer, beat on high speed until cooled (for about 6 minutes).
4. Add the orange extract and food colourings and beat until evenly combined.
5. Prepare a parchment paper-lined baking tray and, using a teaspoon, carefully drop the mixture onto the parchment in dollops not larger than 2½-4cm (1-1½in) across, bringing them to a point at the top.
6. Bake until the kisses are crisp and dry, about 2 hours.
7. Turn the oven off, and let the meringues cool completely in the oven.
8. Dip the bottom of one meringue in white chocolate, and sandwich together with another meringue.
9. Repeat with the remaining kisses.
10. Let the chocolate set before serving.

Almond Bakewell

Queen Victoria's handwritten cookery book records that almond sponge cake was a favourite of Friedrich Wilhelm IV, King of Prussia.

 Serves 6-8

 V

Ingredients

PASTRY

150g (1¼ cup) SELF-RAISING FLOUR
75g (⅓ cup) BUTTER
A little cold WATER

FILLING

370g (13oz) STRAWBERRY JAM
 (or other flavour)
150g (⅔ cup) BUTTER
150g (¾ cup) CASTER
 (TURBINADO) SUGAR
2 EGGS
75g (⅔ cup) SELF-RAISING FLOUR
75g (½ cup) GROUND ALMONDS

DECORATION

110g (4oz) GLACÉ ICING, mixed with
 2-3tbsp WATER to a thick paste
10-12 GLACÉ CHERRIES, cut in halves

Method

1. Preheat the oven to 190°C (375°F).
2. Sift the flour into a bowl and rub in the butter until the mixture resembles fine breadcrumbs.
3. Add water and mix to a smooth dough.
4. Roll out the pastry on to a lightly floured surface.
5. Line a 20cm (8in) flan tin with the pastry, carefully pressing it into the base and sides.
6. Spread the jam on the pastry case.
7. Beat the butter and sugar together until the mixture is light and creamy.
8. Add beaten eggs, flour and ground almonds. Mix well together.
9. Pour the filling into pastry case and bake on the middle shelf for about 25-30 minutes or until golden brown and firm to the touch.
10. When cold, turn out on to a plate.
11. Decorate with glacé icing (simple glaze) and glacé cherries.

How to make Allmond Cakes

Take a pound of Sugar Searced a pound of Allmonds Blanched
beat your Allmonds with Rose Water till they be fine then beat
in your Sugar and when it is done, put in the Whites of 3 or 4
Eggs as you see it in thicknesse, they must be beaten to a
froth, then beat it till it be well mingled then have Ready
your Wafer a Pye Plate and lay it on them into a very
Slow Oven if they doe but Rise it is enough

'How to make Allmond Cakes', Lady Ivory, Lacock Abbey, 1685.

Orange Bakewell

Here is a tasty alternative to the traditional almond bakewell. It was inspired by Ann Talbot's 1745 recipe for 'Oringe Puding'.

Serves 6–8

V

To make an oring puding

Take grated bread, and eggs, and sugar, and spice, as you does for a carrott puding, and cream insteed of milk, take 2 oranges, boyl-d in several watters, till they are tender, and the bitterness taken off, then take out the meat and beat the rind in a morter to a pulp, then mix altogether, and stur in half a pound of melted butter, and bake it with puff past round of dish;

'To make an oringe puding', Ann Talbot, Lacock Abbey, 1745.

Ingredients

FILLING

370g (13oz) MARMALADE, put
    through a sieve so there is no peel
150g (⅔ cup) BUTTER
150g (¾ cup) CASTER
    (TURBINADO) SUGAR
2 EGGS
75g (1¼ cup) FRESH WHITE
    BREADCRUMBS
75g (⅔ cup) SELF-RAISING FLOUR
Juice and rind of 1 large ORANGE
    and pulp of another
A pinch of CINNAMON and NUTMEG

PASTRY

150g (1¼ cup) SELF-RAISING FLOUR
75g (⅓ cup) BUTTER
A little cold WATER

DECORATION

110g (4oz) GLACÉ ICING (SIMPLE
    GLAZE), mixed with 2-3tbsp
    WATER to a thick paste
Fresh orange rind from 3 ORANGES
Pinch of CINNAMON

Method

1. Preheat the oven to 190°C (375°F).
2. Sift flour into a bowl and rub in the butter until
   the mixture resembles fine breadcrumbs.
3. Add water and mix to a smooth dough.
4. Roll out the pastry on to a lightly floured surface.
5. Line a 20cm (8in) flan tin with the pastry,
   carefully pressing it into the base and sides.
6. Spread marmalade on the pastry case.
7. Beat the butter and sugar together until
   the mixture is light and creamy.
8. Add the beaten eggs, breadcrumbs,
   flour, spices, juice, rind and pulp.
9. Mix together well.
10. Pour filling into pastry case and bake on the
    middle shelf for about 25-30 minutes or until
    golden brown and firm to the touch.
11. When cold, turn out on to a plate.

Serving

Decorate with glacé icing (simple glaze), fresh orange rind,
and a little cinnamon.

Alternatively, this recipe can be turned into a delicious
cream dessert by decorating with 500ml (2 cup) of whipped
double cream, the segments of 4 satsumas and a pinch
of cinnamon.

Chocolate Porter Cake

This recipe was inspired by stories of the butler of Castletown House in the mid-eighteenth century, Guinness, who would brew porter for the servants, many years before the world-famous Guinness brewery was founded. It is my very favourite cake.

 Serves 8-10

 V

Ingredients

250ml (1 cup) GUINNESS
250g (1 cup) UNSALTED BUTTER
75g (⅔ cup) COCOA POWDER
200g (1 cup) CASTER
    (TURBINADO) SUGAR
200g (1 cup) DARK MUSCOVADO SUGAR
150ml (⅔ cup) SOUR CREAM
2 large EGGS
1tbsp VANILLA EXTRACT
275g (2¼ cup) PLAIN (SOFT) FLOUR
2½tsp BICARBONATE OF SODA

FOR THE TOPPING

250g (1 cup) UNSALTED BUTTER
500g (5 cup) ICING
    (CONFECTIONER'S) SUGAR
1tbsp VANILLA EXTRACT
1tbsp MILK

Method

1. Preheat the oven to 180°C (350°F).
2. Grease and line a 23cm (9in) springform tin.
3. Pour the Guinness into a large wide saucepan, add the butter and heat until the butter is melted, at which time you should whisk in the cocoa and sugars.
4. In a separate bowl, beat the sour cream with the eggs and vanilla, and then pour them into the saucepan, whisking in the flour and bicarbonate.
5. Pour the cake mixture into the tin and bake for 45-60 minutes.
6. Leave to cool completely in the tin on a cooling rack.
7. When the cake is cold, turn it out on to a flat platter or cake stand.
8. Lightly whip all the topping ingredients together until the mixture is light and fluffy.
9. Apply generously to the top of the cake, creating lovely deep swirls.

Notes

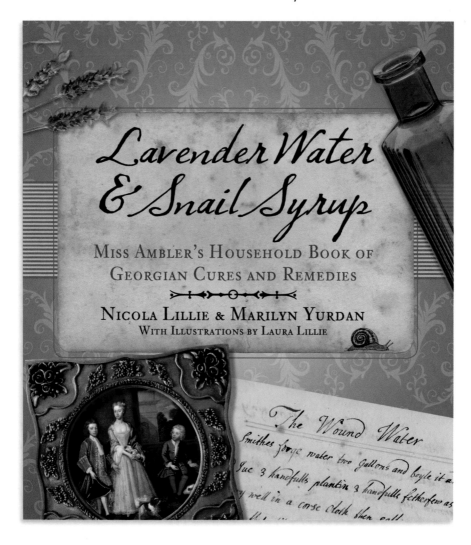